D0330119

Computer Graphics
Primer

by
Mitchell Waite

Howard W. Sams & Co., Inc.
4300 WEST 62ND ST. INDIANAPOLIS, INDIANA 46268 USA

International Standard Book Number: 0-672-21650-7
Library of Congress Catalog Card Number: 79-67129

Illustrated by Robert Gumpertz
Photography by John Werner

Printed in the United States of America.

Preface

Perhaps no single technology has had more impact on people than television. Yet according to the experts the real impact is just starting.

The reason? Home computers that connect to a standard television and convert it into a machine with more raw power than any product ever offered to the consumer and with the capability to completely alter the way we relate to the visual world of electronics.

This book is about one of the most exciting uses of the new home computer products—computer graphics—the ability to create complex drawings, plans, maps, and schematics on the screen of an ordinary black-and-white or color television. It is divided into three chapters. Chapter 1, "Perspectives," presents what the entirely new field of home computer graphics is all about, explains how it got started, and illustrates some of the exciting applications for low-cost graphics displays. Chapter 2, "Basic Concepts," introduces the general hardware and software concepts behind computer graphics and continues by presenting a profile of the numerous products on the market today. A section on graphics accessories is also included.

Chapter 3, the meat of the book, is entitled "Graphics Programming." It introduces the graphics features of the Apple II computer used for this book, and then goes on to describe these concepts: plotting simple equations; drawing lines and vectors; creation of simple geometric shapes (rectangles, triangles, polygons, circles) as well as gaming figures (small tanks, jets, cars, rackets, animals) ; mandalas and other computer art effects, including tunneling; shape shifting, random artwork; detailed drawings and the use of digitizing tables; and, finally, moving figure animation.

The first two chapters of the book can be read any time and will be of help in evaluating which personal computer to buy for graphics work. The third chapter can be studied whether or not you own a computer, but your understanding will certainly be enhanced if one is available to practice the examples on.

The author hopes that you find this journey into computer graphics exciting, comprehensive, and, most of all, enjoyable.

MITCHELL WAITE

To Tony Clemintino

Acknowledgments

The author would like to take the opportunity to give his sincere thanks and appreciation to the individuals and companies who helped make this book a reality:

John Werner for his extremely accurate screen photography
Robert Gumpertz for his warm and happy illustrations
Steve Woznik, Jean Richardson, and Marlen Wightman at Apple Computer, Inc.
Debi Corica, Marketing Dept., Atari, Inc.
Anne Klukas, Bally Consumer Products Division
Joy Baker, Compucolor Corporation
Lora Barrick, Marketing Dept., Exidy, Inc.
Ted E. Naanes, Marketing Support Specialist, Evans and Sutherland
Carl Flock, Product Marketing Manager, Data Treminals Division, Hewlett-Packard
H. L. Siegel, National Publicity and Promotion Manager, Radio Shack
John F. Kadel, Public Relations Manager, Information Display Division, Tectronix, Inc.
Mary Turner, VIP Marketing, RCA
Simon Harrison, Vice President, Axiom Corp.
William Games, instructor, Stockton Unified School District
Leland C. Sheppard, consultant
Ron Denchfield, Section Manager, Public Relations, AMI.
Keith Sutton, Marketing Manager, Digital Engineering Inc.
Barry Millett, Marketing Manager, Matrox Electronic Systems Ltd.

Bob Flexes, President, Digital Graphics Systems
Melvin Goldstein, Marketing Manager, Eclectic Corp.
Robert W. Loewer, President, Micro Diversions, Inc.
Rod Schaffner, Marketing Manager, Digital Computer Products, Houston Instrument, Inc.
Jim Lloid, George Hessler, Talos Systems, Inc.
Lisa Kelly, Promotional Writer, Calma, Inc.
Dan Garza, Manager-Press Relations, Consumer Products Group, Texas Instruments, Inc.
Alfred J. Nucifora, Executive Vice President, Director of Account Services, Cecil West & Associates, for Chromatics, Inc.

Contents

CHAPTER 1

PERSPECTIVES 9

What Is a Graphics Computer Anyway? — What's Been Going
on? — What Is Possible Today? — How Hard Is It to Get Into
Graphics?

CHAPTER 2

BASIC CONCEPTS 25

Stroke Graphics and Raster Scan: The Old and the New —
The Graphics Computer — Memory-Mapped Video: The Scan-
ning Game — The Character Generator ROM — Expanding a
ROM for Character Graphics — Non-ROM Graphics — Ad-
ding Color to the Display — The Ultimate Color Graphics
Display — Memory Partitioning — High-Density Display
Hardware — Evaluating Color, Density, and Screen Format
— Graphics Software and Language Statements — Vector
Graphics Statements — Shape Graphics — Pseudo-Graphics
— Product Profiles — Graphics Accessories — Digitizing Ta-
bles — Digital Plotters — Digital Cameras — Image Digi-
tizers — Retro-Graphics — Graphics Screen Dump Printers
— Hardcopy TTY Graphics — At the Cutting Edge

CHAPTER 3

GRAPHICS PROGRAMMING 101

Introduction to the Apple — Plotting — Line Drawing —
Simple Geometric Shapes — Gaming Figures — Mandalas and
Computer Art — Writing Pong Games in BASIC — Detailed
Drawing and Digitizing Tables — Moving Figure Animation

APPENDIX A

COMPUTER GRAPHICS MANUFACTURERS 174

APPENDIX B

SCREEN COMPARISONS 177

INDEX 180

chapter 1

Perspectives

Rod leaned slightly forward, his eyes intently fixed on the screen before him. He pressed a small pen to the surface of a special digitizing table sitting in front of the computer. On the screen appeared the image of a logic element used in circuit schematics. As he moved the pen along the surface of the table the logic gate element floated out of the menu area and followed his movements on the screen, just as if the gate had been "captured" or hooked by the pen. The logic gate could be moved anywhere on the screen by his simply tracing the pen across the table. Amazing!

Next, when Rod had seemed to find the right place for the gate, he pressed the pen down gently on the table and the gate froze in place on the screen. Rod moved another gate up from the menu area and placed it next to the first. Rapid movements followed and soon wires appeared connecting the gates together. Finally the schematic diagram of a flip-flop circuit emerged on the screen, complete with lines indicating inputs and outputs in proper sequence.

Rod leaned back. A satisfied grin spread across his face as his partner stared wide-eyed in disbelief. "I see it but I don't believe it," his partner said.

Fig. 1-1 shows what Rod's partner had witnessed: the creation of a complex schematic diagram on a low-cost graphics computer. What made this schematic special was that no paper was ever used, no erasers, no whiteout, no ink, and no cutting. Everything was done on the screen of a low-cost computer. A special digitizing table allowed Rod to input his movements to the computer. A program in the computer created the logic elements on the screen and allowed them to be moved from a menu area into a drawing area, then fixed there while wires were drawn from one point to another. A logic element could be rotated and moved elsewhere in seconds. Erasing was possible by simply reversing the drawing color to black.

(A) Setup of equipment.

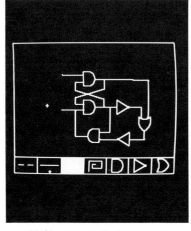
(B) Closeup of display screen.

Courtesy John Werner

Fig. 1-1. Creating schematic diagram by computer.

Sound like the future? Well it's not; in fact this very system can be purchased today, complete with drawing and design software, for under $1500. And you can learn to use it in less than an hour.

This book is about this and other aspects of the latest hobby and consumer market to sweep the nation—personal computer graphics, a new form of visual experience that utilizes low-cost personal computers in ways never before dreamed of.

WHAT IS A GRAPHICS COMPUTER ANYWAY?

It is a new breed of computer that can draw pictures on the screen of a television in ways up to now never imagined. It is a product that is available to the consumer today for under $1000. It can draw intricate pictures from simple programmed instructions or from pen movements on a special digitizing table. It can make a shape grow from a tiny, hardly visible point to a shape larger than the screen. It can rotate shapes through 64 different angles of a complete circle in a fraction of a second. It can draw in eight different colors. It can draw the floor plan of your house faster than you can blink an eye, or it can just as easily plot the path of an orbiting satellite.

Personal computer graphics is a new activity that has developed around the numerous low-cost personal computers on the market today. Before the appearance of the personal computer there was no computer graphics, or, to be more exact, the buying public had no access to computer graphics. Occasionally we saw computer graphics effects in movies and television commercials. Or perhaps we saw a magazine cover with a computer design. Meanwhile, university and corporate scientists, engineers, and technicians were having all the fun playing with these powerful machines.

WHAT'S BEEN GOING ON?

The list of uses for computer graphic applications is for all practical purposes endless. To appreciate this consider the following examples of typical applications by end users of computer graphics equipment.

At NASA, for example, designers have created computer simulations of the actual flight of experimental aircraft. All aspects of the flight are programmed into the computer. Everything the pilot would see out the window of a real aircraft appears on the crt screen of the computer (Fig. 1-2). Safe at the display console a pilot can try difficult landings knowing that a crash simply means running the program again.

Fig. 1-2. Computer-simulated landing field.

Courtesy Evans and Sutherland

Recently NASA has used computer graphics to perfect the motions of the new Space Shuttle so it can maneuver with an attached telescope. (See Fig. 1-3.)

On the architectural front, computer graphics are used to help design complex building structures on the crt screen.

Fig. 1-3. Simulating space shuttle with telescope.

Courtesy Evans and Sutherland

Using special graphics controls the designer can maneuver the positions of the structures anywhere in three-dimensional space, even upside down. Special graphics programs allow the designer to manipulate perspective and scale to show the structure as if it were being viewed from a helicoper. See Fig. 1-4.

How does computer graphics help people care for their health? With new whole body scanners medical investigators are using computer graphics to view the complex parts inside the human body. The computer is fed information from a special scanner that circles around a person lying on a table. Once this information is inside the computer, a graphics "program" constructs a three-dimensional image of any part inside the body on the screen and in full color. (See Fig. 1-5.)

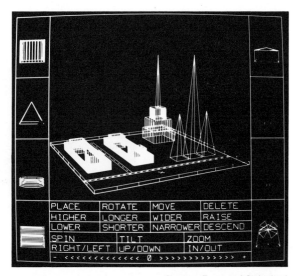

Courtesy Evans and Sutherland

Fig. 1-4. Architectural structures can be moved about.

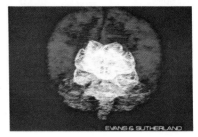

Fig. 1-5. Internal organs may be represented from any viewpoint.

Courtesy Evans and Sutherland

From the display console the researcher can rotate the image, change its color, and even go inside it and look outwards. Such powerful devices allow researchers to probe the inner mysteries of the human body.

Motion pictures have begun to use some of the fantastic graphics technology. For example, in the movie *Star Wars* the scene in which the rebel pilots are briefed on the workings of the "Death Star" was done completely on a graphics computer. (There is a rumor circulating that Bally's new home computer uses a graphics language modeled after the one used to make the Death Star scene.)

The poor artist, however, has had little exposure to the capabilities of graphics computers. Only a specialized group of professionals with skills in computers, art, and engineering have had an opportunity to play with computer graphics (Fig. 1-6).

Fig. 1-6. Artists may utilize computer graphics.

Courtesy Evans and Sutherland

Now that personal computers have dropped in price so as to be no more expensive than a good stereo system, thousands of people are discovering the incredible potential that can be had with these devices. Soon we will see computer graphics being used in ways never before possible.

WHAT IS POSSIBLE TODAY?

The things that can be done with graphics-oriented home computers cover so many possibilities that it would take a separate book to describe them. Therefore we will touch on the most obvious uses, with a reminder that we are just scratching the surface of a deep and complex subject.

Education

Unquestionably the most noticeable effects of low-cost graphics computers will be in education. To understand this, consider that a major factor that makes a scientist great is the ability to visualize a complex idea. For example, some of the world's most honored mathematicians had an incredible ability to see intricate structures in their "mind's eye." What does this have to do with graphics computers?

Consider using a graphics computer to help teach a calculus class. The instructor would set up the graphics program so that students would see a mathematical function (curve) on the screen of the computer. Next the program would approximate the curve with straight-line segments, then start to make the segments smaller and smaller until they reach the limit and perfectly match the original curve. The students would "see" the process of differentiation. This graphics technique can be applied to integration, statistics, algebra, mathematical logic, and so on.

Visualizing abstract concepts in physics can be radically enhanced with the graphics-oriented home computer. For example, the orbits of planets can be traced out so students can watch the subtle perturbations of the orbit. The flight of a rocket or the flight of a bird can be followed. Electromagnetic fields, and for that matter any kind of field, can be instantly drawn out on the computer. Color can be used to accentuate certain features of the field, or to give it a three-dimensional nature. In fact, if green and violet are used to draw two slightly different views of the same object and then green and violet glasses are used to view the computer screen, a true stereoscopic (three-dimensional) image can be obtained!

In electronic technology and engineering classes the graphics computer can be used painlessly to draw and redraw circuit diagrams as we saw in our introductory example. The inner workings of a pn transistor junction could be dramatically illustrated with flowing electrons, a barrier field, floating holes, impurities, and so on. The flow of electricity could be watched, as could the effects of resistance, voltage, and power.

Ecological interactions can be animated on the graphics computer, and students can study the effects of nature, artificially speeded up or slowed down by the computer program. Modeling the gait and movements of animals is another possible use for the graphics computer. The list is endless.

Industry

Any industrial process that involves a flow of materials can take advantage of computer graphics. For example, in chemical manufacturing the computer can draw a real-time schematiclike picture of the process as it actually occurs. Colored pipes show the flow of materials, temperatures are indicated in color, as well as the position of valves (open or closed), the level of liquids in holding tanks, and so on.

Detroit will soon use computer graphics to simulate all the instruments in an automobile dashboard. Instead of several different gauges, there will be a single liquid-crystal flat-panel display in front of the driver (like the kind used on the new digital watches), and the gauges will be displayed and updated on the flat-panel "screen."

In the electronics industry the graphics-oriented computer is used for generating printed-circuit board patterns, complex

masks for IC chips, or displaying logic waveforms as a digital scope does.

Any industrial enterprise that involves assembly is likely to be enhanced with the graphics computer. For example, a complex plumbing installation can be vastly simplified and easily controlled via a graphics computer. A drawing program could be used with pipe sections, valves, etc., in the menu area.

Computer-aided design can be used not only to help visualize a process but it can get involved in the process itself. In designing a package for a product, for example, the computer can instantly compute the total area of the package and then calculate the cost of the entire module based on material costs. The volume of box, regardless of how irregular, can also be computed to aid in heat flow determinations. A decision that normally would take hours can be made by the designer in just a few seconds of computer time.

Art

The graphics computer opens up a whole new world for the artist, especially in the interaction between the artist and the medium itself. The computer with graphics offers the artist a set of tools unlike any before. For example, there are "joystick" devices that look like airplane control sticks and allow you to move a crosshair anywhere on the screen for inputting drawings and pictures.

Or how about using a "mouse" to input drawings to the computer? The "mouse" is a slang word for a device that looks like a tiny doughnut except the doughnut hole has a small crosshair in it. The mouse is moved along the outline of a drawing and the drawing appears on the screen of the computer.

There are also light pens that the artist can use to draw with. A light pen is used to input information directly through the display screen of the computer. A cord connects the pen to the computer, and circuits in the computer figure out where you have placed the light pen on the screen.

Then there are the incredible special effects that the computer can do to any drawing you input to the screen. The computer can create beautiful mandala patterns that resemble patterns found in nature.

The laws of perspective can be intentionally altered with the graphics computer, allowing custom rules of nature to be defined by the artist. A flatland world can be created or a world with strange alternative dimensions. The choices are limitless.

Fun and Games

If you haven't had an opportunity to play any of the new computer games that exist on the market today then you are surely missing out on the most convincing, palmsweating, and breathtaking evidence of what graphics and home computers are all about. It's not that computer games are anything new; computer science students have been flunking exams for years due to fighting Klingon battle cruisers late into the night on the main computer of the college. What is special about computer games of today is two things: (1) their incredible ability to simulate real-time events, such as the sounds of explosions, a hovering ship, two cars crashing, etc. and (2) their ability to analyze and adjust to the player's performance level. No nonelectronic board game has been made that can rival these abilities.

Perhaps the most popular computer game is "Star Trek." Today on the home computer program market you can purchase at least 20 versions of this popular game based on the tv series of the same name. The most interesting of these games have full-blown animating graphics so you view space through the computer screen, as if the screen were the window of your spacecraft. Strange space objects fly by, spacedust clouds the screen then, suddenly, warning buzzers go off as a battle cruiser belonging to the evil Klingon Empire approaches. You grab your joystick and swerve the ship to the left, right in the sights of your outboard photo torpedoes. One press on the trigger control and the screen fills with bright-colored balls of light darting toward the maneuvering cruiser. There is a momentary stillness as the enemy ship seems to begin to rotate in space, then suddenly you're blinded as the screen flashes brilliant colors and in big letters the words ZAP . . ZAP . . ZAP appear. As the game ends, someone pushes you aside so he or she can get into try to beat your score. This is a good example of an action computer game with real-time special effects.

Other such games with real-time effects like this are the infamous PONG™ or TANK video games,* like the kind seen in amusement parks, beer halls, bowling alleys, etc. The PONG™ games available for home computers feature balls that break the rules of physics, twisting and expanding in midflight or falling like lead.

One of the best features of many of the computer games is the adjustable skill level that the player can set. This means someone just starting out can type in that he or she in a novice, while an experienced player can type in the rank of sergeant or general.

Most of the traditional games have a computer counterpart. For example, chess, checkers, and backgammon have all been computerized. One commercial version of chess draws the men on the screen just as they look printed in the newspaper, moves them automatically from one square to another, and allows you to set in the IQ level of the machine to mimic an intelligence level of from 1 to 8.

There are sports games like BASEBALL that let you swing a baseball bat via a joystick control when the computer pitches you a ball. Outfielders scramble about, trying to catch your whopper, while you sweep across the bases towards home plate.

The educational computer games are on the way to altering the entire nature of how our children learn. Today there are games like US MAP, where you must identify states and capitals. The computer draws the outline of the state and gives

---

* PONG is a tradename of Atari, Inc.

geographical drawing hints in full color (that is, if you need them). There are interesting and fun math drill programs that display a math problem on the screen, such as 25×0.5, and you must enter your best estimate of the answer. The computer then throws a dart towards a bullseye target, striking it with an accuracy proportional to that of your estimate. Such drill programs perfect your child's math skills because the math becomes just a side effect of the game.

Finally we have "know yourself" entertainments like LIFE EXPECTANCY, which charts how long you will live given a specific lifestyle; or we have PSYCHOTHERAPY, which will analyze your feelings and behavior to figure out how mentally stable you are!

Again, the list of uses for the graphics-oriented computer in entertainment is endless and limited only by the imagination.

HOW HARD IS IT TO GET INTO GRAPHICS?

It's easy to get started. You can buy a graphics-oriented home computer and teach yourself in a few weeks. There are products as inexpensive as $249, while others cost up to an average of about $800. You could easily spend up to $2000 if you go for the best of the home computers that feature graphics. You could postpone your purchase, because prices will surely drop in the next few years and by then computers will do more, *but* (and this is a big "but") you'll also miss out on a lot of the fun.

A more cautious way to begin is to visit a computer center and play some games on various personal computers there that feature good graphics effects. When you think you're interested in learning how some effect in the game is created, you can get the manual for the product and a listing of the program, and then study both until the creation of the effect becomes clearer.

Today most computers for the home consumer are programmed in the BASIC language. To create your own programs you need to learn how to use simple graphics "instructions" that are provided as part of this language. Although you need to know more about BASIC to complete a complex graphics function, in some applications your knowledge can be minimal due to the simplicity of the graphics instructions. In other words, the graphics function you wish to accomplish may be so simple that little programming expertise is required.

The best way to approach learning graphics is by tying it into an existing project you are already turned on about. For example, if you're into electronics you may wish to develop a 24-trace digital storage scope for designing and troubleshooting computers. You could use a graphics computer to draw the traces on the television that were picked up by your custom interface. If you're into astronomy you might wish to computerize a starmap and have a microplanetarium in your bedroom. If you like playing with the stock market you could get a high-resolution computer to spit out accurate Dow Jones reports just like the graphs in the newspaper.

Courtesy Apple Computer, Inc.

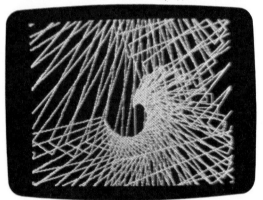

Courtesy Apple Computer, Inc.

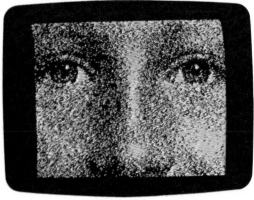

Courtesy Apple Computer, Inc.

Fig. 1-7. Other uses

Courtesy Apple Computer, Inc.

Courtesy Apple Computer, Inc.

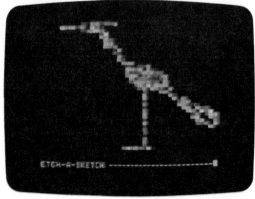

Courtesy Personal Software™

of computer graphics.

Of course, if it's games you enjoy you can start now by thinking of how wonderful your favorite game would be on the computer with full-color graphics, sound, and moving figures.

However you decide to start, keep in mind that there are literally thousands of computer programs already written and available for you to play with on your computer. In fact it may turn out that you'll spend so much time playing the new games that you never find time to write your own. Fig. 1-7 is just a sampling of the things we will learn about in this book. All of these effects were run on the author's personal computer. In the next chapter we will take a look at some of the important concepts you should understand before you buy a graphics computer.

chapter 2

Basic Concepts

Of the hundreds of personal computer products on the market today, only a handful are especially suited for graphic displays. Moreover, each computer has a unique way of handling graphics (remember there is no standard). For example, in the popular PET 2001 computer there is a set of 64 special graphics characters that can be used to draw and plot with. On the other hand, the Apple II computer has no graphics characters but a rich variety of graphics statements that allow you to control any dot in a 280-by-193 screen matrix.

Which is right for you? The answer depends on what your eventual goals are for the computer, how much money you wish to spend, how much effort you can make in learning, etc. In this section we will examine the distinguishing features of the graphics computers of today and we will see how to tell them apart and what makes them tick. We will also look at the elementary hardware techniques for generating a graphics display. A profile of graphics computer products on the market today will be presented. In addition we will examine the various graphics accessories that one can buy today. So let's get started.

STROKE GRAPHICS AND RASTER SCAN: THE OLD AND THE NEW

In the early years of computer graphics the main display device was *not* a standard television screen but rather an expensive cathode-ray tube (crt) like the kind found in oscilloscopes. Like an oscilloscope, the display had an X and Y input. Signals sent to these inputs will move the electron beam in the crt to a point proportional to the amplitudes of the input signals. We call such a display technique *stroke graphics* because the display is sent voltage point pairs and the beam draws a line in one stroke from the last point to the current point. See Fig. 2-1A. This is also called *vector graphics.*

In stroke graphics we need a computer to generate the points that define the shape to send to the display and an expensive digital-to-analog converter (dac) to convert these digital points to voltages for the crt. Since the dac contains complex analog circuits that must be trimmed periodically and since it contains temperature dependent components the stroke graphics method is favored only when money is no object. Of course you can build a low-cost stroke graphics display using 8-bit dac's but it will never compete with the digitally derived displays.

The most popular method for graphics displays today takes advantage of the fact that there are literally hundreds of millions of television sets in the world. All television sets rely on a technique called "raster scanning." In raster scanning the crt beam is deflected in a weaving pattern that sweeps across the screen and down many times per second as shown in Fig. 2-1B.

A television broadcasting station sends a signal to the television that contains special synchronizing pulses. Circuits in the tv use the "sync" pulses to get in step with the transmitted signal. There are horizontal sync pulses for starting the horizontal sweep of the beam and vertical sync pulses for starting the vertical trace of the beam. In between these sync pulses is the video information, also in the form of pulses, that makes up a single horizontal line on the display screen. There are up to 512 of these lines on the tv screen. Up to 1024 points can be defined on a single one of the 512 lines. See Fig. 2-1C.

Most of the time the beam is off. If the computer is properly synchronized to the sweeping beam it can turn it on at any point in the display's X,Y plane and thus form a dot there. The raster scanned television screen can thus be imagined as a superdense matrix of about 1024 dots by 512 lines that is sent to the tv line by line. Thus if the beam is turned on at specific locations on the screen we get a shape made of tiny points. This all may seem even more complex than stroke graphics, but it turns out that raster scanning seriously reduces the need for analog circuits and allows a totally digital display to be built. On the minus side, raster scanning means we must store all the dots that make up a shape rather than

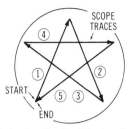

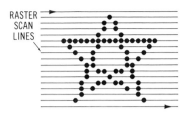

Stroke Graphics: Here five X,Y point pairs define the shape so little memory is required. However, expensive analog circuitry raises cost.

Dot Matrix on Raster Scan: More memory required to store points for shape, but can be built with cheap digital computer logic.

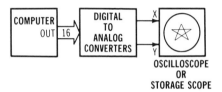

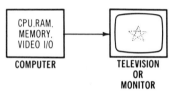

In stroke graphics D/A converters are expensive and slow, computer is overburdened with refreshing display, doesn't work with existing TVs, an so on....

In dot matrix raster scan graphics, low-cost RAM memory and digital video logic work without any adjustment on regular television sets.

(A) The old way: stroke graphics.

(B) The new way: dot matrix raster scan.

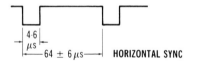

Individual horizontal and vertical sync signals

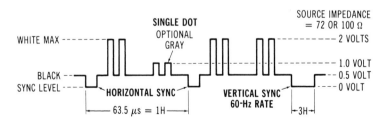

(C) Combined horizontal and vertical sync pulses and video signal form composite signal that can be transmitted over long distances with a single 75-Ω coaxial cable.

Fig. 2-1. For the record—stroke graphics vs. raster scan graphics.

just the end points of vectors as in stroke graphics. This means much more memory. However, since memory is being halved in price every year, raster scanning has become the best approach to low-cost graphics displays. Furthermore, there are tricks that designers can use to make a digital raster scan display act just like a vector graphics display, as we will see.

THE GRAPHICS COMPUTER

All computers that use raster scanned video contain the basic elements shown in Fig. 2-2A, namely a microprocessor, a

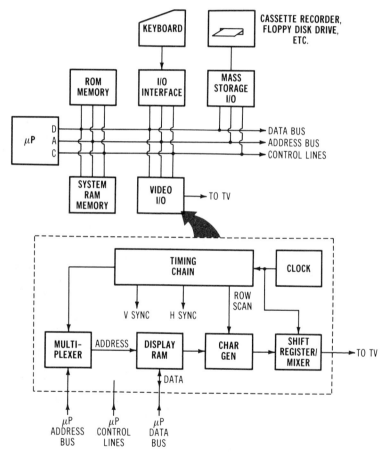

(A) Hardware of typical memory-mapped video circuit (board).

Fig. 2-2.

bus, ROM and RAM memory, keyboard i/o, mass storage i/o, and, most importantly, a video i/o section. The video circuit is expanded in the figure to show its basic components. We will study these later in more detail.

All graphics computers start with some way to get text information such as letters and numbers on the screen—the circuits for graphics then grow around this. A popular technique for getting letters and text (and later graphics) on the television screen is called *memory-mapped video*. The screen output of a memory-mapped video display board that plugs into any S-100 computer and outputs to a high-performance monitor is shown in Fig. 2-2B. Note that the various dashed areas are special "windows," where each receives the output from a specific source.

MEMORY-MAPPED VIDEO: THE SCANNING GAME

In order to display text information on a computer screen we need some way to represent symbols and characters in the

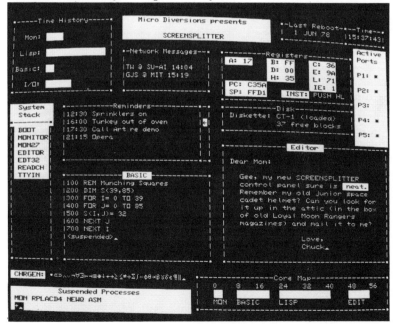

Courtesy Micro Diversions, Inc.

(B) This example of a memory-mapped video display has 40 lines and 86 characters per line.

Memory-mapped video.

computer. Historically, all letters, numbers, and special symbols of the alphabet are coded in computers so each character is a unique 6- or 7-bit value called an *ASCII byte*. (The number of bits used depends on whether the lowercase is included in the character set.) In order to display the ASCII characters, circuits must be built that convert these bit-coded characters to images on the screen. Furthermore, the characters on the tv screen must be refreshed every 1/30 of a second in order to appear permanent to the eye.

In memory mapping a special area of the computer system's RAM is set aside to be the "screen" memory, that is, an area of memory devoted entirely to holding the ASCII characters that will appear on the screen display. Fig. 2-3 illustrates the memory-mapped concept.

As you can see, each location on the screen for a character corresponds to a specific byte number in the long chain of screen memory. Usually the memory is arranged in a simple fashion so each row of characters on the screen corresponds to a series of contiguous bytes in memory. It is important to

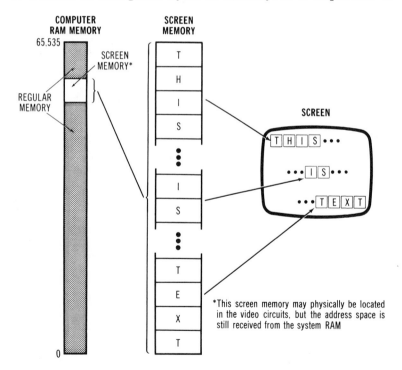

*This screen memory may physically be located in the video circuits, but the address space is still received from the system RAM

Fig. 2-3. In memory-mapped video the screen memory is part of regular RAM.

understand that the part of the system's RAM used by the display can still be used like any other memory, but the computer will convert the bytes in the memory to equivalent ASCII characters and put them on the screen.

THE CHARACTER GENERATOR ROM

Most computers today use a special device called a *character generator ROM* to convert the ASCII bytes to a tiny dot matrix pattern for displaying on the tv screen. This dot matrix can have a density ranging from 5 × 7 (the most coarse and not allowing lowercase) to 10 × 12 (the most dense and allowing all symbols of the alphabet). As the resolution of the dot

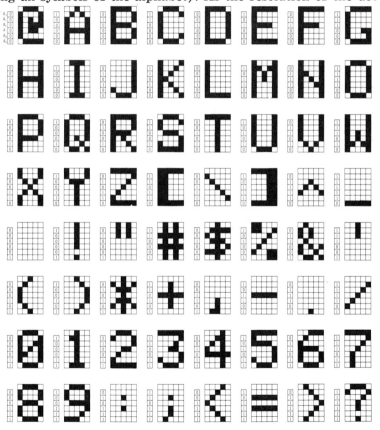

(A) The 5 × 7 ASCII character font from 2513 character generator ROM.

Fig. 2-4. Popular character fonts.

matrix of the character increases so does the cost of the ROM chip; so the 5 × 7 and 7 × 9 matrixes have become popular, the 7 × 9 in Fig. 2-4B having uppercase, lowercase, and Greek math symbols. Besides cost, another factor that limits the character matrix density is maximum dot frequency permitted by the tv. This simply means that the internal circuits of the television set will not allow a dot pattern to be resolved if there are frequency components in it which exceed about 6 MHz.

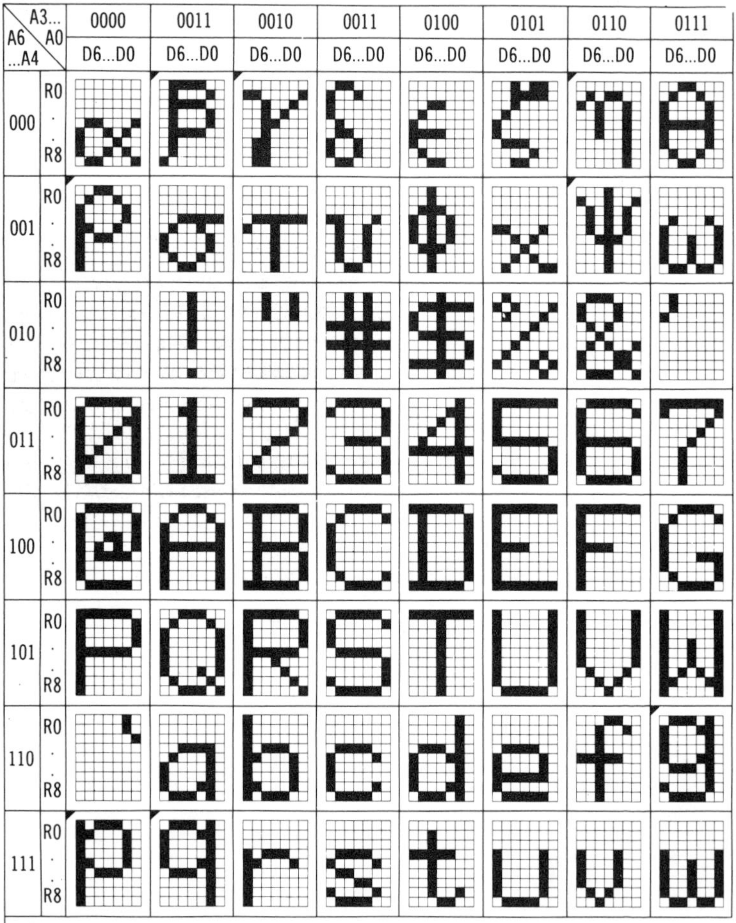

◤ = Shifted Character The character is shifted three rows to R3 at the top of the font and R11 at

(B) The 7 × 9 character font from 6571 character generator ROM.

Fig. 2-4 cont'd. Popular

The basic trick to making a memory-mapped display work is shown in Fig. 2-5. The large switch shown to the left of center in the figure represents circuits that scan the bytes in the screen memory and send them to the character generator ROM.

The purpose of the character generator ROM is to accept the ASCII bytes from memory and convert them to a row of dots for the character that these bytes represent.

1000	1001	1010	1011	1100	1101	1110	1111
D6...D0	D6...D0	D6...D0	D6...D0	D6...D0	D6...D0	D6...D0	D6...D0

the bottom.

character fonts.

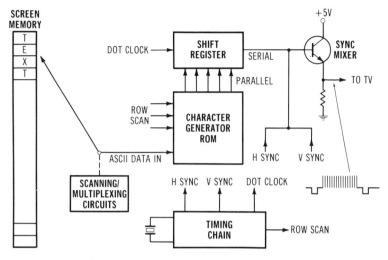

Fig. 2-5. Basic functions of a video display circuit.

The secret to understanding how the video circuits work is to realize that the ROM puts out all the dots for one row of all the characters on a single line of text on the screen (which might be 25 to 80 characters long. This is shown in Fig. 2-6. In this figure the top row of dots of *all* characters on the first line are being displayed. Each row here takes 63 μs. Characters in a line are presented to the ROM eight times, once for each row.

Thus each character on a line of text is accessed from screen memory several times until all the rows are laid down. If the characters are on a 5 × 7 matrix then each character is accessed seven times, one time for each of the seven rows. The more rows in the character matrix, the better and faster the video circuits must be.

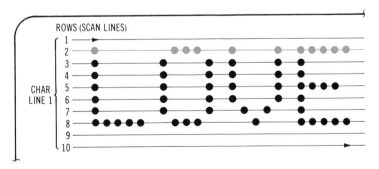

Fig. 2-6. The 5 × 7 dot matrix characters are laid down a row of dots at a time.

Referring back to Fig. 2-5, the box labeled TIMING CHAIN generates horizontal and vertical sync pulses just like the kind the broadcasting people generate, along with a row scan signal for the character generator ROM and a high-frequency dot clock signal for driving the shift register. The shift register takes the parallel row of dots from the ROM and converts it to a serial bitstream called the *raw video*. The transistor is a simplified version of a mixer which adds the horizontal and vertical sync to the raw video. Since everything is digital all signals can be synchronized to the high-frequency dot clock and we get a rock-solid display.

Fig. 2-7 shows a typical low-cost character generator ROM called the 2513. It lacks lowercase and therefore uses only 64 of the 128 ASCII characters. This is why there are only six character inputs to the ROM (two raised to the sixth power is 64). The three remaining inputs (A1, A2, A3) generate the seven row addresses for the characters in the ROM. The dot clock shifts the latched word out serially to form the video data stream.

A complete video display circuit block diagram is presented in Fig. 2-8. Here we see that the timing chain (the five boxes on the left) must keep a count of the character cell, row (cell line), and line. In addition the figure shows the multiplexer, which allows either the video circuits to scan the RAM and

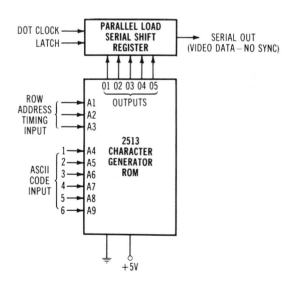

Fig. 2-7. A 5 × 7 row-scan uppercase-only character-generator ROM feeding parallel load shift register.

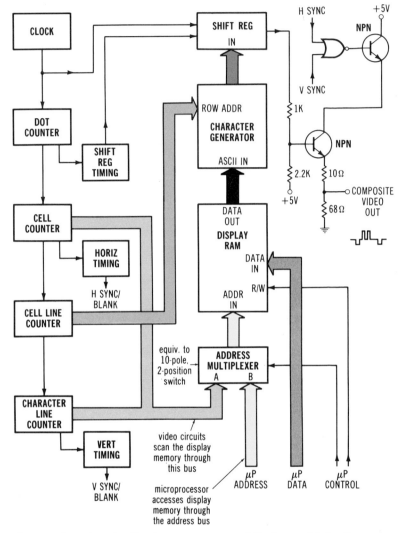

Fig. 2-8. Complete details of a memory-mapped display containing its own display RAM (so it doesn't require any system RAM).

put data on the screen or the computer to access the screen memory to write new data or sometimes to read old data.*

---

* You may wonder what is the maximum number of characters you can squeeze (display) on a standard television set. The fact that the best home computers on the market today that output into a standard television set display a maximum of 64 characters on a single line, with 16

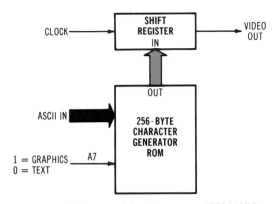

(A) Adding more ROM for graphics characters. (IMSAI VIO example).

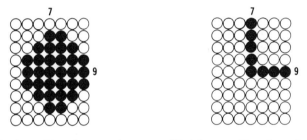

(B) A block graphics character in a 7 × 9 dot matrix.

(C) A line graphics character in a 7 × 9 dot matrix.

Fig. 2-9. How the character generator ROM can contain graphics characters.

EXPANDING A ROM FOR CHARACTER GRAPHICS

The most basic way to add graphics features to the computer is by defining a new set of graphics characters in a larger ROM. A graphics character is the same size as a regular text character. As shown in Fig. 2-9A a 256-byte ROM

---

lines total, may tell you something. If the bandwidth of the television if strip is approximately 6 MHz, then *the maximum number of dots per line* (without blurring of dots) is 63 μs × 6 MHz = 378 dots. Using a 5 × 7 dot matrix for the characters, with one "un-dot" column to separate adjacent characters, gives 6 horizontal dots per character and means a maximum of 378/6 = 63 characters per line. Stretching this to 64 characters is okay but a slight blurring of the dots will begin. To get 80 characters on a single line and 24 lines (i.e., an 80 × 24 screen) using a 7 × 9 dot matrix (upper and lower case) requires 80 × (7+1 un-dot) = 640 dots per line. And 640/63 μs $\cong$ 10 MHz. A custom crt monitor is required to provide this high a bandwidth and this is why most 80 × 24 crt terminals have built-in crt's.

can be used instead of the 64-byte 2513. The ROM has eight address inputs, labeled A0–A7. The A7 line is used to switch in a set of 128 graphics characters or a set of 128 text characters ($128 + 128 = 256$).

This is the approach used in computers like the PET. In the PET a symbol of the graphics character is scribed onto the keyboard key just above the letter on the key. The graphics characters act just like any text symbol and appear when you strike the key and at the same time a special graphics upper-case key.

The format for the graphics characters is usually defined by the design engineer and is burned into the ROM. Therefore you will find no exact standard here, except of course the standard created by the number of PETs sold (estimated at 25,000 in 1978). However, within most graphics character sets you will find what are called *block* graphics characters (Fig. 2-9B) and *line* graphics characters (Fig. 2-9C). These characters can be used to build up complex figures and shapes but these feats of construction require some ingenuity on the part of the programmer.

NON-ROM GRAPHICS

It is not necessary to add more ROM just to get graphics characters on the screen. For example, in Fig. 2-10 a simple modification to a 2513 character generator ROM results in each text character having an equivalent pseudo-block graph-

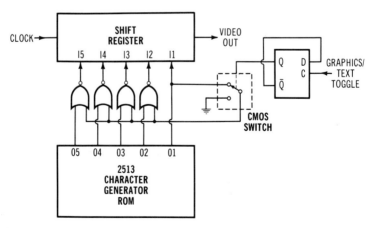

Fig. 2-10. Supersimple text-to-graphics encoder puts a white box in character all for ASCII "0" input, and a blank box for ASCII space.

ics character. The four NOR gates in the drawing will pass the row dots from the ROM without change if the control inputs to the gates are grounded. If the O1 output of the ROM is fed to the gate inputs, we will get a block graphics character whose configuration depends on the ASCII code sent to the ROM. However, the resolution of such a display is not as good as the previous circuit that used an extended ROM graphics set.

The flip-flop in Fig. 2-10 is used to toggle the display between graphics and text. Obviously with this kind of display we cannot have mixed graphics and text.

ADDING COLOR TO THE DISPLAY

Adding color to a display can be done with a programmable color subcarrier generator like the one in Fig. 2-11. Color information is added to a tv signal by inserting a burst of high-frequency signal on the "back porch" of all the horizontal sync pulses (see Fig. 2-11A). This color "burst" is exactly 8 cycles at 3.579545 MHz. The phase of the color burst, rather than the frequency, is made to vary with the original color information. When the color burst phase is compared to a reference signal with a fixed phase the phase changes are converted back to the original color changes for the display. This is called *color encoding* and *decoding*.

Fig. 2-11B shows the actual circuit for a simple color encoder. The important thing to realize about color is that it **requires memory, that is, the color for a particular location on the screen is encoded in bits of memory just like characters are encoded. That is why in the figure there are three** color select inputs to the 4512 1-of-8 decoder. The three color bits are decoded from an ASCII character, and enable one of the eight CMOS delay buffers. These three color inputs are tied indirectly to the computer memory and use the incoming character bytes to enable a particular tap on the delay line set up by the six CMOS inverters. The oscillator generates the required 3.579545-MHz color burst signal and the hex inverters produce the desired delays. Once a phase delay is selected by the 4512, it is passed to the video combiner, where it is added to the raw video and sync signals.

In Fig. 2-12 the circuitry for an 8-color display is shown. Note we are using our NOR gate block graphics/text modification to the character generator ROM. Each ASCII character is converted to a block graphics character and the upper three bits determine the color of that particular character.

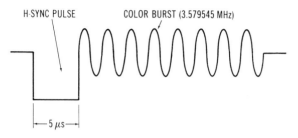

(A) 8 cycles of 3.579545 MHz added to the back porch of horizontal sync pulse.

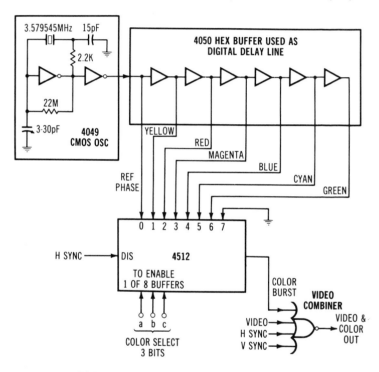

(B) Programmable color subcarrier generator.

Fig. 2-11. Adding color to computer display.

THE ULTIMATE COLOR GRAPHICS DISPLAY

Not to be caught sleeping, the semiconductor industry has carefully watched the way the computer manufacturers build video displays. Using the theory that anything done in LSI is a better deal than the same thing done with random logic,

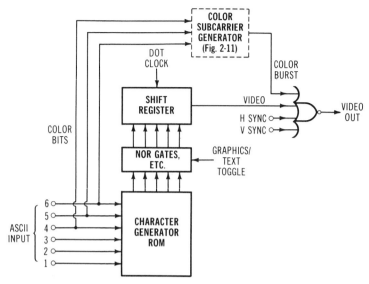

Fig. 2-12. A simple eight-color display.

American Microsystems has developed an incredible video display generator LSI chip called the 68047 vdg.

This is one of the most sophisticated chips on the computer market—generating 64 character ASCII alphanumeric characters with an internal ROM, uppercase and lowercase ASCII via external ROM, two semigraphics-mode block graphics in a 64 × 32 or 64 × 48 matrix with up to eight colors, and eight full graphics modes from 64 × 64 in four colors all the way up to 256 × 192 in one color. This chip generates a composite video display on standard NTSC compatible black-and-white or color television. Fig. 2-13 shows a block diagram of the 40-pin 68047 chip and Fig. 2-14 shows what the display looks like for the eight-color semigraphics mode.

As you can see in the block diagram of Fig. 2-13 the chip contains everything needed for a full-color display in one package. A full-blown graphics computer built around this chip is shown in Fig. 2-15. Here we see that a 6800 microprocessor is used as the main processor and a 6820 PIA (peripheral interface adapter) is used to control and access the 68047 vdg chip. A 9K dynamic RAM memory is used as display memory and an external RAM is used to hold an extra character set. An rf modulator allows going into the tv antenna terminals directly.

Note the $\overline{FS}$ output on the 68047. This is a signal that indicates the chip is in the vertical retrace period. This is coupled

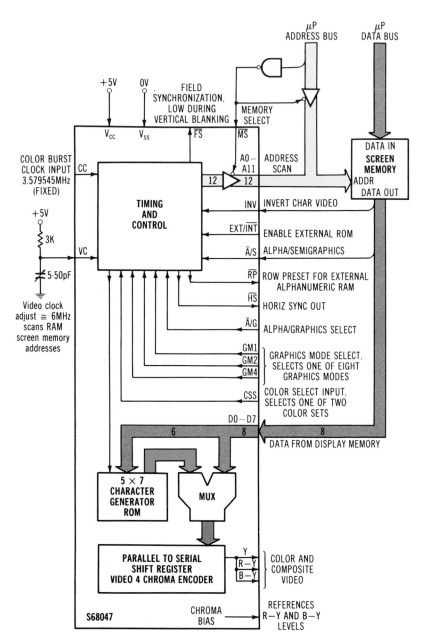

Fig. 2-13. A 68047 video display generator.

Fig 2-14. "Honest Abe" was produced with the AMI 68047 video display generator chip in the eight-color semigraphics mode.

into the $\overline{\text{IRQ}}$ interrupt input on the 6800 microprocessor so that once every vertical retrace period the 6800 microprocessor is interrupted to update the display RAM with new information or to compute new data. When the display is busy it scans the display RAM and sends the information in it to the tv.

Motorola makes a similar chip called the MC6847Y (interlaced) or the MC6847 (noninterlaced). An evaluation board, containing all the necessary hardware to build a complete color graphics display for the 6800 series of microprocessors, is available from Motorola, Inc. It is called the Micro Chroma 68 and is a good way to go if you are interested in designing and experimenting with your own color graphics hardware.

A color graphics board based on the 68047 chip from AMI that is designed to work with any S-100 bus computer is available from Biotech Electronics in Ben Lomond, California. It's called the BCG-800. An intelligent color graphics board based on the Motorola MC6847 (called the CGS-808) is also available from Biotech for S-100 owners. It has firmware packs that allow several graphics subroutines to be executed, including point plot, line draw, cursor read, direct memory transfer, etc. All data transfers are through two i/o ports, allowing fast parallel processing of display and computer.

MEMORY PARTITIONING

In the case of displays that work like the 68047, the screen, depending on the resolution, is divided into a matrix or grid of tiny color squares or dots. Each dot on the screen occupies a particular bit in a byte of screen display memory. The color of a particular dot is also encoded in bits of the display RAM. This encoding of dots and color is called *memory partitioning*.

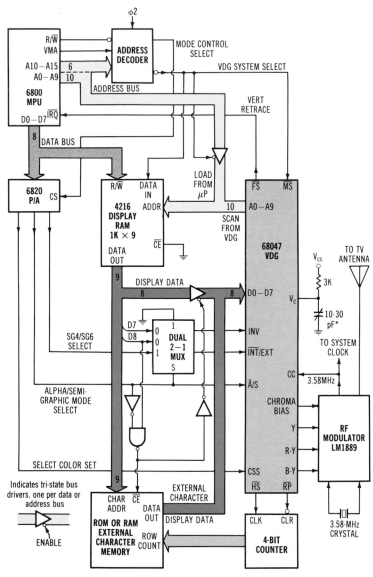

Notes: SG4 = 32 × 16 boxes, 2 × 2 elements per box, 8 colors plus black
SG6 = 32 × 16 boxes, 2 × 3 elements per box, 4 colors plus black

*V_c trimmer sets address scan rate from vdg to display memory

Fig. 2-15. The ultimate color graphics display using the 68047 vdg chip.

Fig. 2-16 shows how the 68047 partitions memory for the 10 different text and graphics modes. As you can see from the drawing as the density of the display increases, more bytes are required to hold the entire screen and this results in a more costly computer product. This figure is a detailed description of how the vdg partitions its display memory. The highest resolution is Graphics 7, with 256 columns by 192 rows. Here 6144 bytes of RAM are required. Each bit in the data word from display RAM specifies a single location on the screen, which may be one color (green or blue). One level down, Graphics 6, uses the same number of bytes, cuts maximum columns to 128 (from 256) but any one dot may be one of four colors. Your software could be assembly or BASIC.

HIGH-DENSITY DISPLAY HARDWARE

There are several approaches to increasing the density of a graphics display. Fig. 2-17 shows the block diagram of a 256 × 256 dot graphics video display made by Matrox, a Canada-based firm. This company makes plug-in video displays for many of the computers on the market, including the popular hobby S-100 and Intel SBC buses. The display in Fig. 2-17 is for S-100 or SBC bused microprocessors using the 8080 or Z-80 chip. With raster scan dot matrix, we can easily mix in text from a separate alphanumeric video board. The X and Y registers are ports for loading with 8-bit coordinates for dots. The third port turns the dot on or off. This unit is the Matrox ALT-256**2. Fig. 2-18 shows screen output from the ALT-256**2 board running in a IMSAI 8080 computer. As seen in the block diagram of Fig. 2-17 the Matrox unit uses port addressing, which means the display is fed X,Y point pairs through its input ports from the 8080. Thus no display RAM is required. Text can be mixed in from a separate alphanumeric board.

The secret to how this circuit works is a single 65,536-bit dynamic RAM memory chip which simply stores all the points on the screen that are *on* as logic 1s and everything that is *off* as logic 0s. The X and Y bytes are fed to the display and the memory address multiplexers use them to locate the proper bit and store it in the memory. Meanwhile the RAM chip is scanned constantly and its output is sent to the screen.

Fig. 2-19 shows a Mona Lisa painting that has been reproduced by using three Matrox ALT-256**2 devices and a special video digitizing camera. There are three bits of gray scale in this photo, and each Matrox board processes one of the

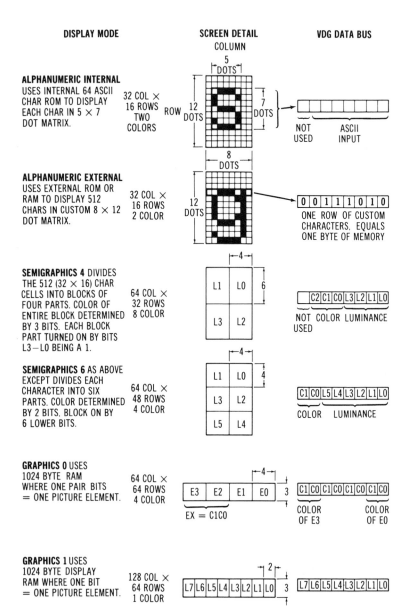

DISPLAY MODE	SCREEN DETAIL	VDG DATA BUS

ALPHANUMERIC INTERNAL
USES INTERNAL 64 ASCII CHAR ROM TO DISPLAY EACH CHAR IN 5 × 7 DOT MATRIX.

32 COL × 16 ROWS TWO COLORS

COLUMN
5 DOTS
ROW 12 DOTS, 7 DOTS

NOT USED   ASCII INPUT

ALPHANUMERIC EXTERNAL
USES EXTERNAL ROM OR RAM TO DISPLAY 512 CHARS IN CUSTOM 8 × 12 DOT MATRIX.

32 COL × 16 ROWS 2 COLOR

8 DOTS
12 DOTS

0 0 1 1 1 0 1 0

ONE ROW OF CUSTOM CHARACTERS. EQUALS ONE BYTE OF MEMORY

SEMIGRAPHICS 4 DIVIDES THE 512 (32 × 16) CHAR CELLS INTO BLOCKS OF FOUR PARTS. COLOR OF ENTIRE BLOCK DETERMINED BY 3 BITS. EACH BLOCK PART TURNED ON BY BITS L3−L0 BEING A 1.

64 COL × 32 ROWS 8 COLOR

L1 | L0   6
L3 | L2

C2 C1 C0 L3 L2 L1 L0

NOT USED   COLOR   LUMINANCE

SEMIGRAPHICS 6 AS ABOVE EXCEPT DIVIDES EACH CHARACTER INTO SIX PARTS. COLOR DETERMINED BY 2 BITS. BLOCK ON BY 6 LOWER BITS.

64 COL × 48 ROWS 4 COLOR

L1 | L0   4
L3 | L2
L5 | L4

C1 C0 L5 L4 L3 L2 L1 L0

COLOR   LUMINANCE

GRAPHICS 0 USES 1024 BYTE RAM WHERE ONE PAIR BITS = ONE PICTURE ELEMENT.

64 COL × 64 ROWS 4 COLOR

E3 | E2 | E1 | E0   3
EX = C1C0

C1 C0 C1 C0 C1 C0 C1 C0

COLOR OF E3   COLOR OF E0

GRAPHICS 1 USES 1024 BYTE DISPLAY RAM WHERE ONE BIT = ONE PICTURE ELEMENT.

128 COL × 64 ROWS 1 COLOR

L7 L6 L5 L4 L3 L2 L1 L0   3

L7 L6 L5 L4 L3 L2 L1 L0

Fig. 2-16. The 68047 vdg

DISPLAY MODE	SCREEN DETAIL	VDG DATA BUS

GRAPHICS 2 USES 2048 BYTES OF DISPLAY RAM WHERE TWO BITS = ONE PICTURE ELEMENT.

128 COL × 64 ROW 4 COLOR

GRAPHICS 3 USES 1536 BYTES IN WHICH ONE BIT = ONE PICTURE ELEMENT.

128 COL × 96 ROW 1 COLOR

GRAPHICS 4 USES 3072 BYTE RAM IN WHICH TWO BITS = ONE PICTURE ELEMENT.

128 COL × 96 ROW 4 COLOR

EX = C1C0

C1|C0|C1|C0|C1|C0|C1|C0

GRAPHICS 5 USES 3072 BYTE RAM IN WHICH ONE BIT SPECIFIES ONE PICTURE ELEMENT.

256 COL × 96 ROW 1 COLOR

L7|L6|L5|L4|L3|L2|L1|L0

GRAPHICS 6 USES 6144 BYTES OF RAM IN WHICH ONE PAIR OF BITS SPECIFIES ONE PICTURE ELEMENT.

128 COL × 192 ROW 4 COLOR

C1|C0|C1|C0|C1|C0|C1|C0

E3   E0

GRAPHICS 7 USES 6144 BYTES OF RAM IN WHICH ONE BIT SPECIFIES ONE PICTURE ELEMENT.

256 COL × 192 ROW 1 COLOR

NOTE THIS IS MAXIMUM RESOLUTION

L7|L6|L5|L4|L3|L2|L1|L0

display memory partitioning.

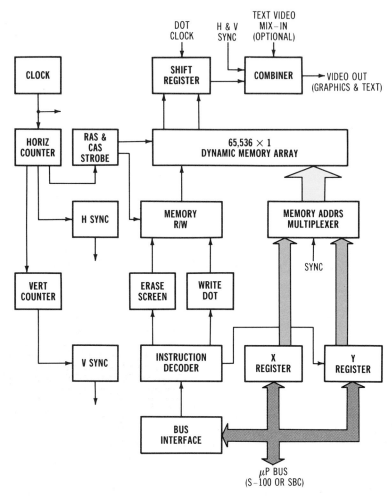

Fig. 2-17. A 65,536-bit Pixel display using port addressing.

three bits. The outputs of the three boards are then summed and sent to the video monitor.

EVALUATING COLOR, DENSITY, AND SCREEN FORMAT

From the previous discussion of hardware it should be apparent that the distinguishing features of any graphics computer display are: the maximum density of the display matrix, the way text and graphics are mixed on the screen, and

Fig. 2-18. Screen output for Matrox Alt-2562 graphics board features resolution of 256 × 256 and into S-100 8080-based computer.**

Fig. 2-19. Digitized Mona Lisa using eight levels of gray per Pixel and three Matrox ALT-2562 boards.**

whether or not color is provided and, if so, how many colors. In the following sections we will examine these important features in the light of real products on the market.

Color

Perhaps no other feature is as motivating as color. Some computers, such as the Apple II, allow a screen element to be any one of 16 different colors. Contrast this with most computers that only allow black and white. The colors offered do

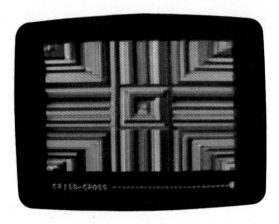

Courtesy Apple Computer, Inc.
Fig. 2-20. This mandala display was produced by an Apple II running in the low-resolution color mode.

not necessarily cover the entire spectrum (some are shades of the same color) but they do allow very interesting and stimulating effects, like the mandala pattern shown in Fig. 2-20 or the Probability Machine shown in Fig. 2-21.

Screen Density

The *density* of a computer display refers to the maximum number of accessible screen elements in the display matrix. Screen density is usually given as the number of horizontal elements by the number of vertical elements in the display, or $H \times V$. Sometimes it is described as X by Y, or columns by rows. Screen density affects the kind of detail possible in graphics displays. The range of densities in graphics computers today is enormous and one has to be most careful when reading manufacturers' claims about density. For example, some manufacturers claim to offer a density of 512 by 256 elements but when looking closer we find that only an 8 by 8

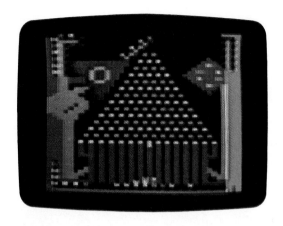

Courtesy Apple Computer, Inc.

Fig. 2-21. The Probability Machine is another example of what can be done with color.

portion of this matrix is accessible. In other words, if a single dot in the total display is to be changed then we must also change (or at least access) up to 63 dots around it. Other displays are not like this and allow any dot in the matrix to be accessed. There are, of course, limits to the density a standard tv will allow with rf modulator entry and this is somewhere around 512 dots horizontally and 256 lines vertically. As you get into expensive monitors, higher frequencies and hence higher densities are possible.

Typical densities for low-cost graphics computers run from 40×25 (PET 2001) to 280×193 (Apple II). In the lower-density computers, graphics characters are usually provided and these have enough detail to make the display look like the density is a lot higher. It is, however, real work to use such displays (as we shall see).

Screen Format

Screen format tells us the number of rows and columns in the text matrix and how the text characters are mixed in with the graphics. Ideally, we would like to be able to mix text anywhere on the graphics screen. In reality, totally mixed graphics coupled with very high screen densities are rare features to find together. For example, the Apple II computer provides a text scrolling window at the bottom of the graphics matrix. Up to four lines of text can be output to the window. Furthermore, the window can be relocated to places other than the bottom of the screen (such as a side column window).

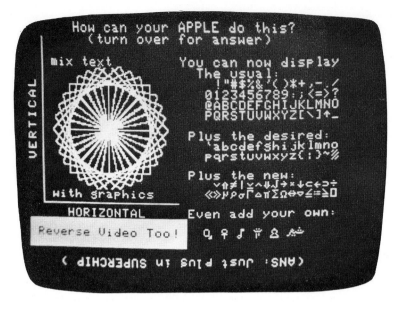

Fig. 2-22. Screen output from Apple II equipped with Superchip shows mixed graphics, rotated characters, and custom character fonts.

But you cannot mix text characters right in with graphics (such as for labeling objects). There is a company, however, that sells a special ROM chip you can plug into the Apple to make it do this and other things. As shown in Fig. 2-22 the chip allows the Apple to rotate letters upside down or sideways. The chip also allows you to create your own custom characters for fancy text effects.

On the computers with lower density (PET, TRS-80, etc.) the text characters can easily be mixed in with graphics because a text character is the same size as a graphics character. However, you have to be careful in the TRS-80 because the smallest accessible screen element using SET and RESET is one-sixth the area of a text character so you could wipe out your graphics with a text character wrongly placed.

GRAPHICS SOFTWARE AND LANGUAGE STATEMENTS

In case you haven't already guessed, how easily we can draw things on the screen is greatly affected by the types of program instructions the manufacturers provide for manipulating screen elements. Today most graphics instructions are part of the popular BASIC language. BASIC is a very simple computer language to learn and there are many good books available to learn it from.*

The language statement provided for controlling the screen can be as elementary as SET x,y, which on the TRS-80 turns a screen element located at x,y ON (white), or COLOR=n, which on the Apple II sets the color to one of sixteen colors (n=0–15). On the other hand, the statements can be extremely sophisticated and powerful like the Apple's HPLOT x1,y1 TO x2,y2 statement, which draws a vector line from x1,y1 to x2,y2, or the Bally's BOX x,y,a,b statement, which places a box of any dimension at any location on the screen, or the Apple's ROT= statement, which rotates a predefined shape on the screen through one of sixty-four rotations.

VECTOR GRAPHICS STATEMENTS

Without a doubt the ability to draw lines from one specified point to another is a powerful feature in the graphics language. Statements of this type are called *vector graphics*. An example is the Apple's HPLOT TO statement. Without this in your version of BASIC you have to use a plotting statement imbedded in a FOR . . . NEXT loop, with the limits of the loop set by the beginning and ending points of the line—messy. Computers which offer vector graphics are the Apple, Compucolor, and Matrox.

SHAPE GRAPHICS

Sometimes in graphics we would like to be able to create some sort of figure that could be controlled from a BASIC program. For example, we might wish to create the drawing of a pattern and then make it expand, contract, rotate, and so on. This can be done on graphics computers which feature shape graphics as part of the BASIC language. An example would be the Apple's shape tables and the statements DRAW n AT x1,y1, ROT=, and SCALE=. This feature is invaluable when you are using the computer to create highly detailed images or when you want to use the screen as a menu and move shapes with a light pen or digitizing pen.

---

* See, for example, Mitchell Waite and Michael Pardee, *BASIC Primer*, Indianapolis: Howard W. Sams & Co., Inc., 1978.

PSEUDO-GRAPHICS

On the very low cost graphics computers, such as the RCA VIP, a sort of pseudo-graphics command language is provided which, although slightly abstract, allows very good display effects.

PRODUCT PROFILES

In order to help make an intelligent decision when purchasing a graphics computer product, the following product profile charts are provided. These describe the salient features of the various graphics computer products on the market. These features include who makes it, how much it costs, true graphics resolution, number of colors, graphics characters, and a listing of graphics language statements (if provided). The author's subjective impression of the product is given under a comments heading. For the reader's own perspective the profiles are divided into two parts: low cost and high cost.

Low-Cost Graphics Computers

These are personal computers for the home, lab, or office in the $250 to about $1500 price bracket. Unless otherwise stated the cost figure assumes there are 16K bytes of RAM and that mass storage is a cassette tape recorder. The meaning of the numbers under the heading CODE indicates:

1 = monitor or television required
2 = cassette tape recorder required
All-in-one = self-contained system, no accessories required

APPLE II

Company	Apple Computer, Inc.
Product	Apple II
Cost	$1200 w/16K RAM $1700 w/16K RAM & disk
True Graphics	280h × 193 hires (high resolution = 54,040 dots)
Resolution	40H × 48v lores (low resolution)
Indirect Dot Resolution	N.A.
Number of Colors	8 hires 15 lores
Number of Graphics Characters	Up to 255 custom graphic characters in shape tables
Graphics Statements	lores GR, COLOR=, PLOT, HLIN, VLIN, SCRN hires HGR, HGR2, HCOLOR=, HPLOT, HPLOT TO, SHLOAD, DRAW, XDRAW, ROT=, SCALE=

Comments   The Apple II computer was the first of the true graphics computers for the home, and this has enabled it to acquire a firm foothold in the market and an enthusiastic group of Apple II owners. The Apple II requires a color television or monitor. A supermachine and the only computer to offer high-resolution vector graphics statements.

Code   1, 2

ATARI 400

Company	Atari, Inc.
Product	Atari 400
Cost	$550 w/8K RAM (nonexpandable)
Graphics Resolution	40h × 24v to 320h × 192v (6 graphics modes)
Indirect Dot Resolution	N.A.
Number of Colors	2 colors in highest resolution 4 colors in lowest resolution 8 levels of luminance (brightness)

Number of Graphics Characters	In text mode works like the PET, giving 30 keyboard-accessible fixed graphics characters. These may be used in PRINT statements in BASIC.
Graphics Statements	GRAPHICS X; PLOT X,Y; DRAWTO W,Z; COLOR X; SETCOLOR X.
Comments	The Atari computers (see the Atari 800 on next page) are sort of a mixture of the best of the Apple II, PET 2001, and the TI-99/4. The Atari's graphics statements in BASIC allow vector line drawing, but no "shape" graphic statements exist, as found in the Apple II's high-resolution package.* Color control is quite nice, allowing up to four colors at the same time and eight brightness levels for each color! Sound control and paddle manipulation on the Atari are superb. Like TI, Atari offers plug-in ROM cartridges for languages, such as BASIC, and for application programs. Some game application programs provide incredible three-dimensional motion, but the user is locked out from using this feature at this time. Like TI, Atari doesn't believe most educators are, or want to be, programmers. Hence there is a trade-off against providing advanced graphics features and for providing things complete, perfected, and totally debugged end-user application programs in ROM packs.
Code	1, 2

*There is a rumor that Atari has shape table potential and that 16 color capability is in the works.

ATARI 800

Company	Atari, Inc.
Product	Atari 800
Cost	$999 w/tape recorder and 8K RAM expandable to 48K
Graphics Resolution	Same as Atari 400
Indirect Dot Resolution	Same as Atari 400
Number of Colors	Same as Atari 400

Number of Graphics Characters	Same as Atari 400
Graphics Statements	Same as Atari 400
Comments	The Model 800 is identical to the 400, except it comes with a tape recorder that is program controlled, can hold up to 48K of RAM (the 400 is 8K bytes maximum at this time), and has a better-feel keyboard. Both units have fully passed FCC type approval for rf attachment to any standard television (color).
Code	1

BALLY

Company   Bally Manufacturing Corp.

Product   Bally Arcade Computer System

Cost $330 with 4 joysticks

Graphics Resolution   159h × 87v

Indirect Dot Resolution   N.A.

Number of Colors   Any 2 of 256 (one foreground and one background color)

Number of Graphics Characters   None

Graphics Statements   BOX, CLEAR, ERASE, LINE
FC= (foreground color equals) BC= (background color equals)

Comments   Very low cost, the Bally unit has large selection of preprogrammed games and a good display density. However, a calculatorlike keypad makes programming difficult. The graphics statements are interesting and show that someone special is behind the Bally. Look for incredible improvements in the Bally Arcade soon, particularly a higher-level

unit with a unique graphics language called
GRAFIX.

Code   1

PET 2001

Company	Commodore Business Machines Ltd.
Product	PET 2001 (Personal Electronic Translator)
Cost	$800 with 8K RAM
Graphics Resolution	40h × 25v
Indirect Dot Resolution	320h × 200v (64,000 dots)
Number of Colors	Black and white
Number of Graphics Characters	64 fixed
Graphics Statements	None

Comments   The famous PET set of graphics characters. Integral crt, cassette recorder, and calculatorlike keypad. A nice "one-package" computer and very popular among schools. However, the techniques for using the graphics may be confusing, especially for beginners. There is no direct way to access individual dots on the screen.

Code   All-in-one

SORCERER

Company	Exidy, Inc.
Product	Sorcerer
Cost	$1000
Graphics Resolution	64h × 30v
Indirect Dot Resolution	512h × 240v (122,880 dots)
Number of Colors	Black and white
Number of Graphics Characters	128 fixed and 128 user programmable in RAM
Graphics Statements	None
Comments	Ultimately the highest indirect resolution of any small computer, but unfortunately it is difficult to control from BASIC. Has PET set of graphics characters. However, Sorcerer does

allow user to create custom 8 × 8 cell graphics characters in RAM, which in turn can be used for imaginative graphics, foreign language fonts, etc.

Code   1, 2

INTERCOLOR 8001

Company	Intelligent Systems Corp. (ISC)
Product	Intercolor 8001
Cost	$1500
Graphics Resolution	160h × 192v
Indirect Dot Resolution	N.A.
Number of Colors	8 foreground 8 background
Number of Graphics Characters	None

Graphics Statements	PLOT n (n=0–255) The value of "n" in the PLOT statement sets the mode, the back and foreground color, whether to plot a color square, a line, etc.
Comments	Professional big brother to the Compucolor described next, the Intercolor uses a built-in color crt which results in extremely bright and vivid displays not possible with a color television and modulator.
Code	2

COMPUCOLOR II

Company	Intelligent Systems Corp.
Product	Compucolor II, Model 3
Cost	$1500 with one disk and 8K RAM
Graphics Resolution	128h × 128v
Indirect Dot Resolution	N.A.
Number of Colors	8
Number of Graphics Characters	None
Graphics Statements	Same as Intercolor 8001
Comments	This is ISC's color personal computer and comes with a built-in minidisk drive for mass

storage, and a color crt. Like the 8001, the graphics software is slightly obtuse, but still powerful.

Code   All-in-one

TRS-80

Company	Radio Shack Corp. (a division of Tandy Corp.)
Product	TRS-80 Computer System
Cost	$1000 with Level II BASIC, 8K RAM cassette and monitor
Graphics Resolution	128h × 48v
Indirect Dot Resolution	N.A.
Number of Colors	Black and white
Number of Graphics Characters	None
Graphics Statements	SET X,Y RESET X,Y CLS
Comments	It is a more or less accepted fact that half of the 200,000 computers sold in 1977 were Radio Shack TRS-80s. However, people do

not buy the TRS-80 for its graphics, which are inferior to other computers, but rather because it is the most available, serviceable, supported, and documented product on the market. Considering that the TRS-80 is designed to satisfy many segments of the computer market (educational, business, etc.), the graphics are not all that bad. Rumor has it that a color board for the TRS-80 is coming.

Code   All-in-one

COSMAC VIP

Company	RCA
Product	COSMAC VIP
Cost	$250 with 2K RAM
Graphics Resolution	64h × 32v
Indirect Dot Resolution	N.A.
Number of Colors	Black and white
Number of Graphics Characters	None

Graphics Statements	No high-level language statements but pseudo-assembly CHIP-8 mnemonics perform graphics plotting.
Comments	Has CHIP-8 graphics language in ROM, hex keypad, 1802 CMOS microprocessor. Very good product for the money.
Code	1, 2

TI-99/4

Company	Texas Instruments, Inc.
Product	TI-99/4
Cost	$1150 with 16K of RAM and color monitor
Graphics Resolution	32h × 24v
Indirect Dot Resolution	256h × 192v
Number of Colors	16
Number of Graphics Characters	128 maximum user programmable
Graphics Statements	CALL COLOR, CALL VCHAR, CALL HCHAR
Comments	The TI-99/4 is somewhat a disappointment from a graphics programmer's standpoint. The high-resolution 256h × 192v dot matrix is not directly accessible through BASIC, although characters on an 8 × 8 matrix may be created and stored in RAM. TI does not

allow access to machine language and no PEEK or POKE statements are provided. TI's plan is to sell programmed ROMs—solid-state software—which are complete application programs written in machine language by TI programmers.* These do not use the high-resolution graphics. Obviously TI wants to be the only one writing programs that access graphics at the high-resolution level—too bad. But not to berate the TI unit, it has one operational feature found no where else: a $150 speech synthesizer that contains 256 preprogrammed words. Also a built-in, BASIC-accessible, four-voice music synthesizer which covers 5 octaves and is capable of 30 volume levels.

*A TI spokesperson says the reason for this is that the market as perceived by TI is software driven, meaning people buy hardware based on what software is available. Since most consumers are not programmers, programming features were given up for other benefits.

High-Cost Graphics Computers

These are graphics-oriented computers in the $5000 to $70,-000 price bracket. Although this is far beyond most people's budgets, such computers are accessible to larger institutions, groups, and clubs. The features of these computers are included here because by 1984 the home computers will be identical if not superior!

PICTURE SYSTEM II

Company	Evans and Sutherland
Product	Picture System II
Cost	$68,500
Graphics Resolution	4096h × 4096v × 64 intensity levels
Indirect Dot Resolution	N.A.
Number of Colors	5
Number of Graphics Characters	
Graphics Statements	

Comments   The world's most advanced commercial graphics computer. Allows up to 436 ASCII characters on one line with variable point size from 4 pt to 76 pt.

HP 2648

Company	Hewlett-Packard, Inc.
Product	2648 Intelligent Graphics Terminal
Cost	
Graphics Resolution	720h × 360v (ASCII mode: 37 lines × 80 char/line)
Indirect Dot Resolution	
Number of Colors	Black and white
Number of Graphics Characters	
Graphics Statements	
Comments	Very powerful graphics software on the HP terminal, including viewport and windowing, rubberbanding, ZOOM and PAN, and so on. ASCII mode of 37 lines better than most terminals on the market.

TEKTRONIX 4051

Company	Tektronix, Inc.
Product	4051 Graphic Computing System
Cost	$6000 with 8K RAM, 3M tape drive
Graphics Resolution	1024h × 780v (ASCII mode: 34 lines × 80 char/line)
Indirect Dot Resolution	N.A.
Number of Colors	Black and green
Number of Graphics Characters	
Graphics Statements	
Comments	Storage tube-type crt means selective erase of screen graphics is not possible; however,

this computer offers more dot resolution for the money than anything else on the market. Has powerful graphics software for bar-graphs and piecharts, as well as HP-like graphics commands.

TEKTRONIX 4027

Company	Tektronix, Inc.
Product	4027 Color Graphics Computing System
Cost	$8700
Graphics Resolution	640h × 480v
Indirect Dot Resolution	N.A.
Number of Colors	Any 8 of 64
Number of Graphics Characters	
Graphics Statements	
Comments	Highest-resolution commercial raster scan color terminal on the market. Has software

similar to 4051. This is not a stand-alone system and requires a "host" computer to operate.

CHROMATICS CG SERIES

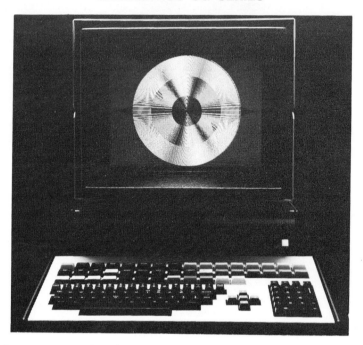

Company	Chromatics, Inc.
Product	CG Series (13-, 15- and 19-inch tubes)
Cost	Approximately $20,000, depending on options
Graphics Resolution	512h × 512v max (85 chars, 51 lines)
Indirect Dot Resolution	N.A.
Number of Colors	8 foreground, 8 background
Number of Graphics Characters	Up to 192 custom defined in an 8 × 10 dot matrix
Graphics Statements	Escape codes, DOT, X BAR, YBAR, Vector, Concatenate Vector, window, CREATE, RE-DRAW

Comments	Chromatics color computers pack the kind of features you would expect in a $50,000 system. Besides its amazing 512 × 512 dot resolution, it has optional hardware for color shading, and superfast hardware generation (normally vectors driven by software). ZOOM and PAN are provided, and the display memory can contain up to 131,092 bytes of dynamic RAM. Four independent windows are allowed. Floppy disk software includes Microsoft extended BASIC, a Z-80 assembler, text editor, and various monitor utilities.

GRAPHICS ACCESSORIES

Lots of interesting accessories exist for helping you do graphics. Some of these devices enhance the way you send or input information to the computer, while others aid in the output side of the graphics. Included here are light pens, joysticks, digitizing tables, digital cameras, plotters, hardcopy screen-dump printers, and so on.

DIGITIZING TABLES

One of the main problems with any high-density graphics display is getting external graphics, such as detailed drawings, photographs, etc., into the computer and on the screen. This is understandable when you consider that a screen like the one for Apple contains over 54,000 dots. One nifty way to handle this is with the digitizing table. A digitizing table is a device that looks like a flat board (Fig. 2-23). A special pen is connected to it through a cable. The table contains electronics that allow it to accurately locate the position of the pen and feed this information to the computer. A program provided with the computer uses the pen information to turn on a specific dot on the screen. A digitizing table is used by placing a drawing on the table and tracing it out with the pen, or just moving the pen on the table as though it were a drawing surface.

The table can send either single point to the computer when the pen is pressed or it can send a continual stream of points as it is held down. This allows fast, fluidlike drawing movements.

Fig. 2-23. A digitizing table allows entering highly detailed information into the graphics computer.

DIGITAL PLOTTERS

A digital plotter is a computer output device which draws curves and other computer graphics data on ordinary 8-1/2 × 11 inch (21.6 × 27.9 cm) paper. See Fig. 2-24.

Data from the computer is translated into signals which cause tiny incremental movements of the plotter's pen. The pen on the plotter (a felt-tip ink pen) is moved by a combination of X and Y carriage motions. The pen can move in eight different directions. These eight directions are used to simulate all the movements necessary to create curves. Since the incremental movement of the plotter is small (0.005 inch or 127μm) proper selection of directional moves combine into what the eye perceives as a smooth curve or line. See Fig. 2-25.

Courtesy Houston Instrument, Inc.

Fig. 2-24. A digital plotter provides up to 200 incremental movements per inch, and requires RC-232C serial or parallel 6-bit TTL data.

Because of the extremely small movements that the plotter can make, drawings on it are very precise and detailed. Fig. 2-26 shows some examples of plots made with the Houston Instrument HI PLOT™ plotter.

Using the plotter from BASIC requires that the output program send the plotter ASCII characters that stand for the incremental directions. For example, to draw a line 0.1 inch (0.25 cm) long in the +X direction the code string "z sp-sp rrrrrrrrrry" is sent to the plotter. The z stands for pen down, sp stands for an ASCII space character, r means move right, and y means pen up.

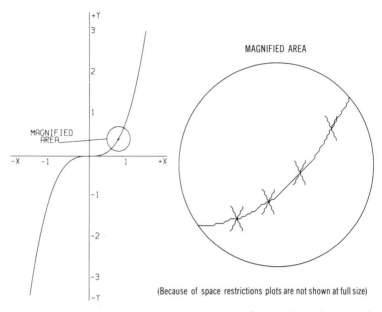

Fig. 2-25. Example of resolution of digital plotter.

DIGITAL CAMERAS

A digital camera is used to take a picture in real time and store it in the computer memory as well as display it on the screen. The camera shown in Fig. 2-27 is a solid-state camera featuring a 100 × 100 bit CCD self-scanning charge coupled image array. This unique camera may be used for visible or infrared viewing and for character recognition. It will operate in a vacuum, under water, at high altitude, or in a magnetic environment because no high voltage or magnetic deflection is used. The camera may also be used for ir surveillance with an ir light source. The display may be used with an X-Y oscilloscope or a video processing system like the one shown in Fig. 2-27.

The video processor consists of three boards: an analog-to-digital converter board, a tv sync and DMA board, and a mother board. It is available from Solid State Sales.

IMAGE DIGITIZERS

An image digitizer is an electronic device that takes video information from any standard source (tv, video recorder,

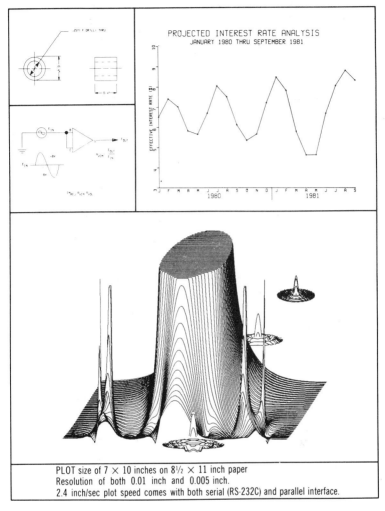

PLOT size of 7 × 10 inches on 8½ × 11 inch paper
Resolution of both 0.01 inch and 0.005 inch.
2.4 inch/sec plot speed comes with both serial (RS-232C) and parallel interface.

Courtesy Houston Instrument, Inc.

Fig. 2-26. Example of output of digital plotter.

computer, camera) and converts the information to digital
bits, stores the bits in the computer memory, and displays the
resulting picture on the display screen. The process of converting the video picture information to digital form requires
expensive high-speed analog-to-digital converters. Fig. 2-28
is a block diagram of an image digitizer called the CAT-100
which provides full-color displays and can convert an entire
picture frame in 1/60 of a second. The tv frame is represented

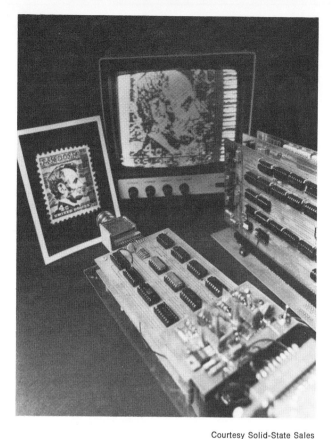

Fig. 2-27. Solid-state digital camera features a 100 × 100-bit self-scanned charge-coupled image array.

as 65,536 numbers of four bits each which are packed in pairs in the 32K-byte image memory. This system is available from Digital Graphics Systems and works with any S-100 based computer.

Figs. 2-29A and 2-29B are examples of the digitized output from the CAT-100. Note the extremely accurate resolution possible with this unit.

RETRO-GRAPHICS

What about adding graphics facilities to an existing nongraphics computer system? Fig. 2-30 illustrates a device that can be retro-fitted into the popular ADM-3A serial terminal to allow full-blown high-resolution plotting and graphing. The device is a pc board that fits inside the ADM-3A case under

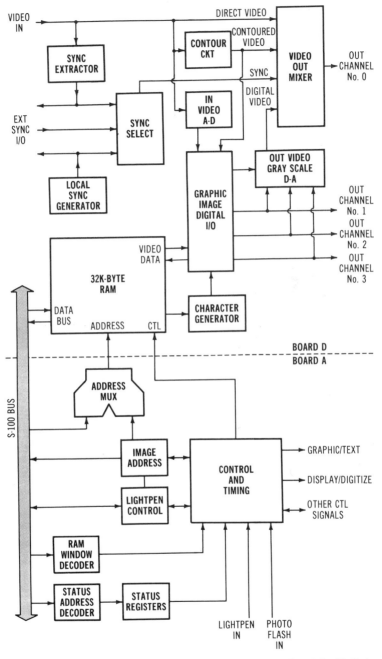

Courtesy Digital Graphic Systems

Fig. 2-28. Block diagram of an image digitizer for S-100 based computers.

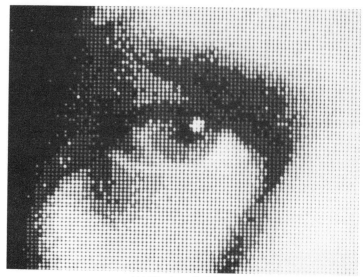

(A) Black and white.

(B) Color.

Fig. 2-29. Examples of digitized output from the CAT-100.

the regular ADM board. It contains a Z-80A microprocessor, with 512 by 250 plotting resolution and a Tektronix software compatibility option. The product is made by Digital Engineering, Inc., in California and is called the RG-512.

Fig. 2-31 shows a block diagram of the RG-512. A special attraction of the device is that it features a vector mode for

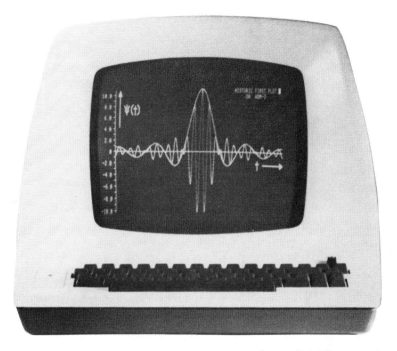

Fig. 2-30. Retro-Graphics RG-512 unit fits inside standard ADM-3A terminal (shown) and allows point plotting and vector graphics on a 512 × 250 matrix.

plotting lines from user-specified end points, a selective erase function so specific vectors can be removed, a point mode, and an annotation mode for mixing in text from the ADM terminal. As you can see in the block diagram, the RG-512 simply mixes its output in with the normal ADM text output so both are passed to the screen.

The actual plotting resolution is just short of amazing and it means very exciting graphics potential for nongraphics computer systems.

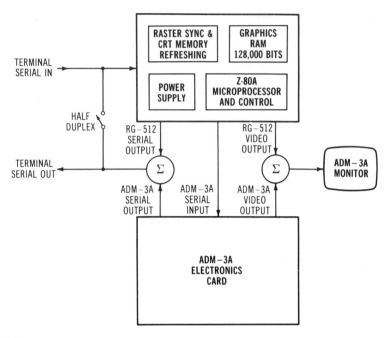

Fig. 2-31. Block diagram of Retro-Graphics 512 × 250 video graphics add-on.

GRAPHICS SCREEN DUMP PRINTERS

One problem with using television screens for displaying graphics is that when the set is turned off, it's bye-bye graphics. What we need is some way to print or "dump" the screen image on paper. Regular printers won't do it because they only handle alphanumeric characters. The solution is provided by Axiom Corporation in Glendale, California, which makes a special printer/plotter that works with the PET, TRS-80, and Apple computers. Called the EX-820 Microplotter, the unit prints out high-resolution graphics plus full ASCII alphanumerics. Shown in Fig. 2-32, it uses special 5-inch (12.7-cm) wide aluminized electrosensitive paper that burns off the top layer of aluminum, which covers an underlying black surface. This results in extremely high contrast characters, unlike anything obtainable on regular paper.

The EX-820 contains its own 8048 microprocessor and firmware for extensive software control. The user can select, via control sequences, three different column widths (20, 40, or 80 characters per column) and three different horizontal dot

Courtesy Axiom Corp.

Fig. 2-32. EX-820 Microplotter can handle full alphanumerics and high-resolution graphics to 512 dots per line.

Courtesy Axiom Corp.

Fig. 2-33. Example of EX-820 output.

Fig. 2-34. Example of screen dump of Muppets created with digitizing table.

resolutions, with up to 512 dots per line. Vertical dot spacing is 65 dots per inch.

Several program listings used in this book were produced on the EX-820. Fig. 2-33 shows a dump of an image plotted on the screen of an Apple II computer. The screen dump was accomplished by simply typing a control R at the keyboard. The total dump took less than 6 seconds.

The EX-820 makes a nice output device for the digitizing table described earlier. Fig. 2-34 shows the image of a drawing made by David Fox at the Marin Computer Center of the popular and lovable Muppets. The digitizing table allowed the image to be perfected on the screen before it was output to the Microplotter.

HARDCOPY TTY GRAPHICS

Not to give the impression that computer graphics always requires a graphics computer, the printout in Fig. 2-35 was produced on a DECwriter teletype printer using a clever BASIC program. The printouts produce a density effect by typing several characters without moving the printhead.

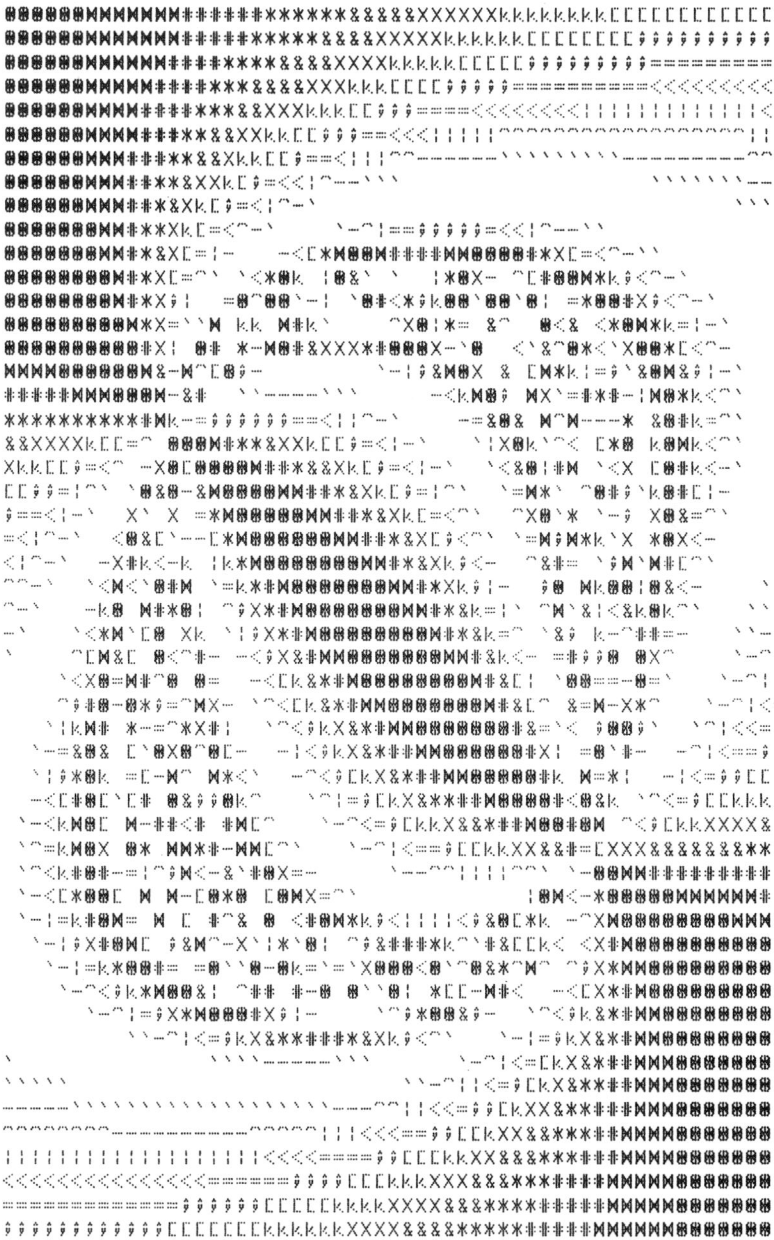

Courtesy William Games

Fig. 2-35. This is a graph of 3-dimensional surface done on a tty printer.

The pattern is a three-dimensional graph of a function, with the Z axis presented as changing density. The program appeared in the November/December 1978 issue of *Creative Computing* and was written by William Games. This kind of program can be expanded for all kinds of special effects, but requires more programmer sophistication than the graphics-oriented computers described previously.

In the next chapter we will examine several interesting and important ideas of graphics programming.

AT THE CUTTING EDGE

If it's true that today's tools become tomorrow's toys, then the prodigy of the Calma GDS-II will certainly be a sight to behold. The Calma GDS-II is a graphics integrated design tool: a 7-color, 20-inch (50.8-cm), refresh display terminal with a high-resolution digitizing table; all this is connected to a Data General Eclipse computer, with floating-point processor and 80-megabyte hard disk. Most GDS-II systems use a Versatec 8242 electrostatic plotter for hardcopy.

From afar the GDS-II looks like the bridge of the starship *Enterprise* (see Fig. 2-36A). But up close, the GDS-II shows its stuff. As shown in Fig. 2-36B the main purpose of the GDS-II is the creation of a database of coordinates that define the layers of an integrated semiconductor circuit. A typical IC design may involve up to 64 layers of individual structures. These structures represent transistors, diodes, resistors, and connecting paths between component parts. With the GDS-II the designer can represent up to 64 different color shadings, and can move through these layers one at a time. The designer can stop on a surface layer and move throughout its plane, a section of the surface may be expanded with a zoom feature and the user may then alter the shape with the aid of the digitizing table.

The Calma unit features a VLSI database of over 4 billion points per axis. Coordinates are entered via the input table; software automatically connects points with 90-degree or 45-degree lines. For hardcopy the user can specify that the color display be reproduced on a high-resolution black and white electrostatic plotter, and, as shown in Fig. 2-37, the colors in the display are converted to equivalent black and white shadings (64 maximum shades).

Software for the GDS-II is truly the graphics designer's dream. Control of the structure on the screen is through the graphics editor. The editor manipulates the database (the coordinates of the structure) and includes these features: erase, move, polygon manipulate, stretch side, group stretch, window, copy, data type, layer change, rotate, mirror, area shift, notch, and close.

(A) Left to right: graphics console, plotter, auxillary terminal, printer, hard disk, and minicomputer.

(B) Showing 20-in, 7-color, raster scanned crt, with 64 color shadings, and designer is selecting functions via digitizing table and is preparing IC design on left.

Courtesy Calma, Inc.

Fig 2-36. The Calma GDS-II system.

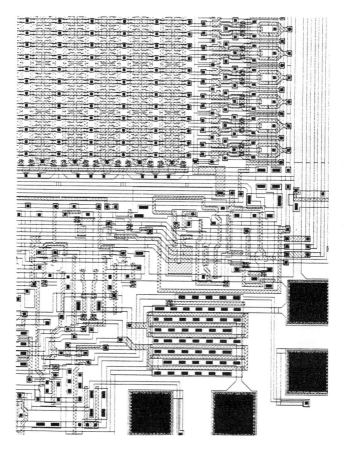

Fig. 2-37. Electrostatic plot of integrated-circuit structures showing semiconductor layers as different shadings.

Besides being used for IC design, the Calma people provide similar packages for architectural design and for mapping (construction of geological maps).

But before you run out to buy a GDS-II you should consider first owning a semiconductor company with revenues of at least $500 million per year, because the price tag on the GDS-II is a healthy $250,000! So far Calma has sold over 20 GDS-II systems and has many more on order.

chapter **3**

Graphics Programming

This chapter describes how to accomplish graphics effects such as plotting equations, line drawing, and animation on the Apple II computer. The ideas here covered, however, are generally applicable to computers that offer vector graphics capability and a fairly dense display matrix (at least 128 × 128).

We will begin this chapter by introducing the graphics features of the Apple II, and then continue with the main ideas of the chapter. So, let's get started.

INTRODUCTION TO THE APPLE

The Apple II computer was chosen for this book for several reasons, the most important of which are its high-resolution 280h × 193v eight-color display, its powerful vector graphics language statements, and its moderate cost (under $1200). Keep in mind that other computers feature vector graphics and dense display matrices (although not as dense as the Apple) and therefore most of the concepts covered here also apply to them.

An exhaustive list of the features of the Apple would be too large for this book, but we can summarize those most important for good graphics work:

- 8-color high-resolution 280h × 193v display
- 16-color low-resolution 40h × 40v display
- powerful vector graphics BASIC statements

- very fast 6502 BASIC in ROM for true animation
- shape tables allow up to 255 shapes
- rotation and scaling commands
- 6502 assembler and disassembler in ROM

Before we jump into using high-resolution graphics to accomplish special effects we need to learn a little about Apple's version of BASIC, the screen format of the Apple, and the graphics statements provided as part of BASIC.

Applesoft

Applesoft is Apple's enhancement of Microsoft's popular floating-point BASIC language. (Microsoft BASIC is *the* de facto standard BASIC used by almost every personal computer manufacturer today, including the TRS-80, PET 2001, Atari, etc.) Applesoft has almost all the standard keywords and features of Microsoft BASIC including its 9-digit arithmetic and a large function library. A complete discussion of Microsoft BASIC can be found in Mitch Waite and Michael Pardee, *BASIC Primer*. In addition to Microsoft's standard features, Applesoft contains a set of powerful high- and low-resolution graphics statements. This book describes the use of the high-resolution graphics statements and assumes you have a minimal knowledge of Microsoft BASIC or a BASIC similar to it. Applesoft is supplied on diskette, cassette tape, or ROM. The ROM version was used in this book.

High-Resolution Screen Format

The format and organization of the Apple's high-resolution screen is shown in Appendix B. The "hires" screen defaults to an organization of 280h × 160v (that is, 280 horizontal columns by 160 vertical rows) with a four-line text scrolling window at the screen bottom. This gives a total of 44,800 dots you can control from Applesoft. The text window can be removed (via a specific POKE instruction) giving a increased graphics format of 280h × 193v, or 54,040 dots. Any line of text in the scrolling window can hold up to 40 characters. Six colors are available for a dot: black, white, violet, green, blue, and orange. Older Apples lack blue and orange in the high-resolution mode.

Graphics Keywords

There are seven keywords, or instructions, that are part of Applesoft and are used especially for hires graphics: HGR, HCOLOR, HPLOT, SHLOAD, DRAW, SCALE, and ROT. The last four, namely SHLOAD, DRAW, SCALE, and ROT are used with Apple "shape tables" and are described later in the book. The first three keywords, HGR, HCOLOR, and HPLOT, are used frequently in high-resolution programs and therefore will be defined and explained first. The definitions of these keywords follow:

HGR

Graphics Mode. Switches the computer into the high-resolution graphics mode, clears the screen top area to black, and provides bottom four lines of text. 8K bytes of RAM memory (Page 1; 8K to 16K) is displayed.

HCOLOR = expr

Set Color. Sets the high-resolution graphics color to that specified by the value of expression (expr),* which must be in the range 0 to 7, inclusive. Color names and their values are:

0 black	4 black2
1 green	5 orange
2 violet	6 blue
3 white	7 white2

On early Apples color 5=green and 6=blue. Black2 and white2 are normally used with orange and blue colors.

HPLOT expr1, expr2

Plot a dot. Plots a high-resolution dot whose x coordinate is (expr1) and whose y coordinate is (expr2). The color of the dot is determined by the most recently executed HCOLOR statement. Expression expr1 must be in the range of 0 through 279 while expression expr2 must be in the range of 0 through 191. An attempt to plot a point whose coordinates exceed these limits causes the ?ILLEGAL QUANTITY ERROR message.

Now you should be prepared to begin your programming.

PLOTTING

To *plot* on a graphics computer is to place a dot or square somewhere on the screen of the computer. The size of the dot, whether it is colored or just black and white, and so on, depend on the type of computer you are using. How you get the dot plotted on the screen also depends on the type of computer. In general, home computers use special graphics instructions to get the dot plotted on the screen. These instructions are called *graphics statements.* Usually they are part of the BASIC programming language of the machine, but in some cases (RCA VIP) they may be assembly language instructions.

As an example, to plot in the TRS-80 we use the statement SET X,Y (where X and Y specify the horizontal and vertical location for the dot on the screen matrix). To remove the dot the statement RESET X,Y is used.

---

* By expression (expr) we mean a constant (5), a variable (Z), or a mathematical formula made up of constants and variables (Z*B+3).

On the Apple II in the high-resolution mode we use the statement HPLOT X,Y to plot a dot. The color of the dot must first be set with the HCOLOR= statement. In the low-resolution mode on the Apple II we use the statement PLOT X,Y to plot a color square on the screen. The color of the square is set previously with the COLOR= statement.

There are several uses for the plot instruction, including the plotting of equations, the drawing of pictures, and so on. Here we will explore the plotting of equations on the Apple in the high-resolution mode.

Plotting Equations

One of the most useful applications of the graphics computer is its ability to plot the graph of a complex equation. Besides removing the drudgery of plotting equations by hand, using the graphics computer to automatically plot allows the viewer to "see" the insides of an equation as it is drawn out onto the screen. For example, imagine plotting the path of a swinging pendulum on the screen, the trajectory of a model rocket, the three waveforms of a biorhythm chart, the delay of a pulse, and so on.

The generation of the graph of an equation is accomplished by simply placing the equation itself inside some kind of a programmed loop, such as a FOR ... NEXT loop in BASIC. The purpose of the loop is to generate values for the horizontal axis (X) and feed them to the equation. The equation then takes these values and produces the corresponding value for the vertical axis (Y). The X and Y pair is then used inside a PLOT statement (or HPLOT or whatever) to make one point of the graph appear on the screen.

A good place to begin for an equation plotting program is with a simple equation for a straight line (see Example 1, p. 105). Recall that the equation for a straight line is $Y=mX+b$.

As you can see the graph of the equation is upside down. This is because on the Apple in high-resolution 0,0 is the upper left corner of the screen and the Y axis extends down the screen to 159.* The X axis extends from zero on the left to 279 on the right.

The graph of the equation can be "flipped" over by simply changing the equation to $Y=159-(3*X+10)$. Since Y must

---

* Although the vertical axis extends to 193, a four-line scrolling text window at the screen bottom eats up rows 160 to 192 in the Apple. A POKE statement can be used to disable the scrolling window and free rows 160–192 for graphics.

Example 1:

Generate the graph of the straight-line equation

$$y = 3x + 10 \qquad (x = 0 \text{ to } 50)$$

on the Apple II in the high-resolution mode.

Solution: ⟶ Switches Apple into high-resolution graphics mode

```
10 HGR: HCOLOR=3 ← Sets color to white
20 FOR X=0 TO 50 ← Start the loop
30 Y=3*X+10 ← Our equation
40 HPLOT X,Y ← Plot it
50 NEXT X
60 END
```

See Fig. 3-1.

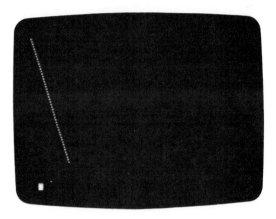

Fig. 3-1. Computer plot of y = 3x + 10 for x = 0 to x = 50.

not exceed 159 or be less than 0 we must restrict the range of X $(0<X<50)$.

Nonlinear equations that form interesting curves are the next logical type of equation to try graphing with a plotting program. See Example 2, p. 106.

Here the magic term X^2 makes the Y values grow faster than the X values and hence a curve is formed. The trick to getting this to work on the computer is to divide the equation by 490 in order to keep Y from growing beyond 159. We can flip the graph over with 30 Y=159− (X^2/490).

Example 2:

Generate the graph of the nonlinear equation:

$$y = x^2 \qquad (x = 1 \text{ to } 279)$$

on the Apple II in hires (high resolution).

Solution:

```
10 HGR: HCOLOR=3
20 FOR X=1 TO 279
30 Y=(X^2)/490
40 HPLOT X,Y
50 NEXT X
60 END
```

See Fig. 3-2.

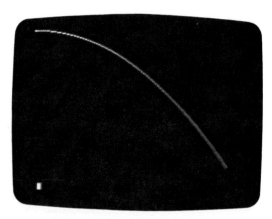

Fig. 3-2. Computer plot of $y = x^2$ for $x = 1$ to $x = 279$.

Harmonic motion, interference, sinusoidal oscillation, and other wavelike phenomena can easily be displayed on the screen of the computer. See Example 3, p. 107.

Here is how the program works. Statement 10 puts us in the high-resolution mode, sets the radius R to 79, and sets the constant two-pi (TPI) to 6.28318. Next we enter a FOR... NEXT loop which produces values of I degrees from 0 to 720. Next in statement 30 we divide I by 2.58 so that X varies from 0 to 279 for the HPLOT statement (remember the rules).

The expression (I/360*TPI) in statement 40 is the formula for converting degrees (I) to radians. The formula is inside

Example 3:

Plot two cycles ($x = 0°$ to $720°$) of the equations:

$$y_1 = \sin x$$
$$y_2 = \cos x$$

on the Apple computer in high-resolution color. Make the curve out of dots and make equation y_1 plot in green and y_2 in violet. Use the slow but simple and effective "brute-force" approach where the limits of the FOR...NEXT loop are in degrees.

Solution:

Radius

```
 10 HGR: R=79: TPI=6.28318            Two pi
 20 FOR I=0 to 720                    Loop makes I=0 to 720
 30 X=I/2.58
 40 Y1=R*SIN(I/360*TPI)
 50 HCOLOR=1: REM   GREEN DOTS
 60 HPLOT X,80-Y1
 70 Y2=R*COS(I/360*TPI)
 80 HCOLOR=2: REM   VIOLET DOTS
 90 HPLOT X,80-Y2
100 NEXT I
```

See Fig. 3-3.

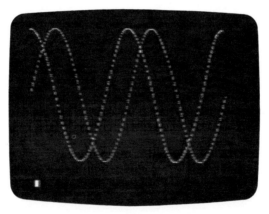

Fig. 3-3. Plot of two cycles of two sine waves.

the SIN function, so we get Y1 to equal to the sine of I degrees, which varies from -1 to $+1$. Multiplying by 79 sets the maximum and minimum peaks for the sine plot of Y1 and Y2. Next we set the HCOLOR to green with HCOLOR=1 and

Example 4:

Plot four cycles of the equation:

$$y = \sin t \qquad (t = -4\pi \text{ to } +4\pi)$$

on the Apple computer in high-resolution color graphics using the "N=number of points" plotting method. Use 180 points for N, and use radians instead of degrees.

Solution:

```
10 HGR: HCOLOR=3: PI=3.14159
15 A1=-4*PI ──────────────── Lower limit in radians
20 A2=4*PI ───────────────── Upper limit in radians
25 N=180 ─────────────────── Number of points
30 R=50 ──────────────────── Radius
35 INC=(A2-A1)/N ─────────── Increment
40 F=279/(A2-A1) ─────────── Factor (multiplier) to get X
45 FOR I=A1 TO A2 STEP INC
50 X=I*F
55 Y=R*SIN(I)
60 HPLOT 140+X,80+Y
65 NEXT I
70 END
```

See Fig. 3-4.

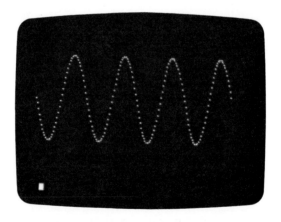

Fig. 3-4. Plot of four sine-wave cycles.

finally the great HPLOT statement : HPLOT X,80−Y1 actually plots the equation Y1 on the screen (naturally turning Y1 upside down with 80−Y1.

Statement 70 generates the cosine of I (which, as electronics buffs know, leads the sine by 90°). Last, the equation of Y2 is plotted by statement 90 and we loop to the next value for I degrees.

Note that the plot in Fig. 3-3 is not smooth. Further, from a time standpoint the program took over 30 seconds to draw out on the screen. This is due to the fact that we are attempting to plot so many points (1440 here).

A much better way to plot a trigonometric function involves specifying the number of points to plot. See Example 4, p. 108.

Here is how this program works and why it is better than the previous brute force program. Statement 10 switches us into graphics, sets the color to white, and sets the variable P1 to 3.14159. Statements 15 and 20 set A1 and A2 to equal the limits of the sine wave in radians (multiples of π). Statement 25 sets N to 180, and statement 30 sets the radius R to 50. Statement 35 then takes these limits and produces the variable INC, which will be used as the step size for the upcoming FOR...NEXT loop! Statement 40 produces the multiplier F that will be used later to generate values of X for the screen from values of I.

In statement 45 we begin the main FOR...NEXT loop that plots out our sine wave. Note the loop limits are A1 to A2 so we can easily put other functions inside the loop and the loop increment is INC. In statement 50 we first produce our value of X for the screen from the loop index I (remember I is in radians and the screen is not). Then in statement 55 we generate our corresponding Y value using the trigonometric SIN function. The variable R multiplies Y to set the "peak-to-peak" size of the function.

Statement 60 is different from previous HPLOTs in that we define the center of the screen to be 140,80 and add the values of X and Y to these constants to get the actual plot point. We can do this because the loop index is in radians and negative values of X and Y are produced from the SIN function.

This program is extremely flexible because we can change so many things so quickly. For example, to add more plotting points simply make N larger in statement 25; or to increase frequency (i.e. add more values on the screen) simply make A1 and A2 larger. See Example 5, p. 110.

Polar Plotting

Plotting equations in "polar" form makes it very easy to plot circles and ellipses on the computer. In fact very beauti-

Example 5:

Increase the frequency (number of crests on the screen) to 12 and increase the number of points N to 720. See how much longer the plot takes.

Solution:

```
10 HGR: HCOLOR=3: PI=3.14159
15 A1=−12*PI  ──────────────── New lower limit
20 A2=12*PI  ──────────────── New upper limit
25 N=720  ──────────────── New number of points
       .
       .
       .
  {as in previous program}
       .
       .
70 END
```

See Fig. 3-5.

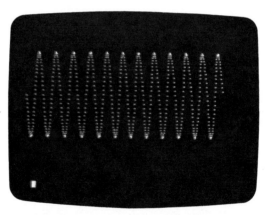

Fig 3-5. Plot of twelve sine-wave cycles.

ful patterns can be generated from polar equations by repeated plotting of the same equation with a slight shift occurring in one parameter. In a polar equation we generate values for an angle in radians (preferably 0 to 2π or $0°$ to $360°$). Then we use the values for the angles inside the function that we wish to plot. Finally, we use a transformation formula to get the proper X,Y values for a Cartesian coordinate system as on the computer screen. The previous sine wave program was close to a polar plot. The next program shows how to form a circle, by a polar equation. See Example 6.

Example 6:

Graph the polar equation for a circle of radius

$$r = 50 \qquad (0 \text{ to } 2\pi \text{ radians})$$

on the Apple in high-resolution color. Use N to specify the number of points as 32.

Solution:

```
10 HGR: HCOLOR=3: PI=3.14159
15 A1=0
20 A2=2*PI
25 N=32
30 R=50
35 INC=(A2−A1)/N
40 FOR I=A1 TO A2 STEP INC
45 X=R*SIN(I)
50 Y=R*COS(I)
55 HPLOT 140+X,80+Y
60 NEXT I
65 END
```

See Fig. 3-6.

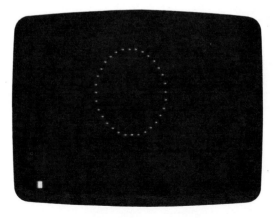

Fig. 3-6. Plot of *r* = 50.

As you can see we almost get a perfect circle. Try the above program a second time, only increasing the number of points to 64, and notice that the dots tend to disappear.

Now, in case you didn't know it, the actual function we plotted in our previous program was the equation $r=50$. What if we change the equation so r is no longer a constant? For

---

Example 7:

Plot the graph of the four-leaf "rose curve" polar equation

$$r = a \cos 2t \qquad (t = 0 \text{ to } 2\pi, \, a = 50)$$

using the relations

$$x = r \sin t \qquad y = r \cos t$$

on the Apple II in high-resolution color.

Solution:

```
10 HGR: HCOLOR=3:PI=3.14159
15 A1=0: A2=2*PI
20 N=90: A=50
25 INC=(A2−A1)/N
30 FOR I=A1 TO A2 STEP INC
35 R=A*COS(2*I)
40 X=R*SIN(I)
45 Y=R*COS(I)
50 HPLOT 140+X,80+Y
55 NEXT I
60 END
```

Conversion from polar to Cartesian coordinates

See Fig. 3-7.

Fig. 3-7. Plot of rose curve equation.

example, we could have $r = \cos t$. What kind of plot do you think will occur? See Example 7, p. 112.

This program is similar to the previous one except we use the cosine function (COS) to generate the value of R. As you can see in Fig. 3-7 the rose curve has four "petals" to it. There are actually whole families of rose curves that can be plotted on the computer. The equations for these can be found in any standard math reference book.

To add more points to the rose curve simply make N in statement 20 larger; to increase the diameter of the curve make A in statement 20 larger. Be careful because the program doesn't check the values of X and Y before they are plotted by statement 50, and if they are too large or too small, an error message will occur.

LINE DRAWING

Another basic way to draw things on the computer involves using lines for these drawings instead of points. Lines are necessary when we wish to draw borders and boundaries, walls, bar graphs, simple geometric shapes, and so on. Certain computers allow you to draw a line anywhere on the screen with only one simple BASIC statement. We say these computers have *vector* graphics capability (the line is a vector). Some of the simple computers require that you make up a line as a series of dots, which is much harder but still possible.

Borders

Let's look at a simple example of how line-drawing statements work. To draw lines on the Apple we simply use a variation of the HPLOT statement called the HPLOT TO statement. Here is the syntax of the statement:

HPLOT x1,y1 TO x2,y2 (TO x3,y3 ..)

where x1,y1 represents the starting location of the line and x2,y2 represents the ending location of the line. The (TO x3, y3...) part means we can continue drawing lines to successive points by just adding more TO xN,yN statements to the main HPLOT. Note that this all assumes the color has been previously set with HCOLOR=. Recall that $0<x<279$ and $0<y<159$. See Example 8, p. 114.

Quite simple, isn't it? The coordinates in the HPLOT TO statement take us in a clockwise rotation around the screen starting at 0,0 and ending at 0,0 again.

Example 8:

Draw a continuous white border around the screen of the Apple using one long HPLOT TO statement.

Solution:

```
10 HGR: HCOLOR=3
20 HPLOT 0,0 TO 279,0 TO 279,159
   TO 0,159 TO 0,0
30 END
```

See Fig. 3-8.

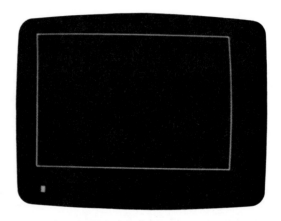

Fig. 3-8. Plot of continuous white border.

Diagonal Lines

Drawing diagonal lines allows us to make simple triangles and similar shapes. See Example 9, p. 115.

Here the first HPLOT statement selects the starting point for the line and then the successive HPLOT TO statements draw the triangle itself. We say the computer remembers the last coordinate location, so the next HPLOT TO statement causes the line to be drawn from this last location.

SIMPLE GEOMETRIC SHAPES

In this section we will examine the techniques for making simple geometric shapes such as boxes, rectangles, triangles, polygons, and circles on the computer. We will also see how

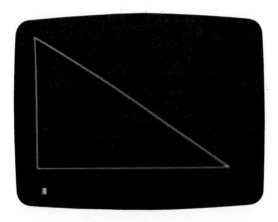
to easily change the size and location of these shapes on the screen by using the concept of relocatability.

Boxes and Rectangles

Drawing rectangles requires that we pick the four corners and place them in an HPLOT TO statement. There are some surprises, however. See Example 10, p. 116.

The first thing we notice is that this isn't a true square, that is, the sides don't look equal on the screen even though we know they are! The obvious reason is that an increment on the X axis is not the same as an increment on the Y axis. This is also true for the circle done previously in Example 6. Here is how to fix this so your shapes are perfect. Take out

Example 10:

Draw a square 100×100 units on the Apple II in high resolution. Center the square.

Solution:

Since we know the screen is 279 by 159 we assume that the center of the screen is 140,80 and thus make the upper left starting corner of the box $140 - (100/2) = 90$ and $80 - (100/2) = 30$.

```
10 HGR: HCOLOR=3
20 HPLOT 90,30 TO 190,30 TO 190,130
   TO 90,130 TO 90,30
30 END
```

See Fig. 3-10.

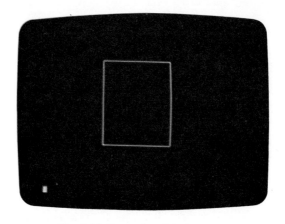

Fig. 3-10. Computer plot of square.

a ruler and measure the sides of the square. This will vary with your particular television set. On one set this was Y=2.5 inches (6.35 cm) and X=2.0625 inches (5.23 cm). Now divide Y by X to get the ratio, here 2.5/2.0625=1.212. This ratio says that one step in Y gives about 1.212 times the same step in the X. Or the Y spacing is about 21 percent longer than the X spacing. The trick now is to adjust our programs by multiplying X by 1.212, or dividing Y by 1.212 just before we do the actual plotting (of course using your own constant ratio).

This is all very nice, but how do we implement the ratio correcting idea into our programs? The way to do this is to make the shape size dependent on a pair of variables. At the same time make the shape's starting location on the screen a variable also. See Example 11.

Example 11:

Draw a square 100×100 units on the Apple II using a correction factor of 1.212 (or whatever your screen is) to remove distortion and make the shape size and the start corner variable.

Solution:

```
10 HGR: HCOLOR=3: F=1.212 ←—— Correction "factor" for your tv
20 XS=100*F
30 YS=100
40 X=XS/2: Y=YS/2
50 I=140: J=80 ←——————————— Screen center
60 HPLOT I−X,J−Y TO I+X,J−Y ←— Variable-size box
   TO I+X,J+Y TO I−X,J+Y
   TO I−X,J−Y
70 END
```

See Fig. 3-11.

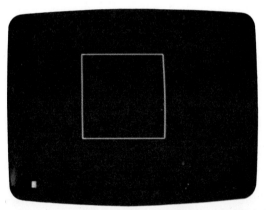

Fig. 3-11. Plot of square with correction factor included.

Although this program is more complicated than the one before it, notice how easy it is to move the square around or change its size. The x side is called XS and the y side is called YS. Statement 20 multiplies XS by F, our correction factor. Statement 40 makes X and Y equal to one-half the size of the x and y sides. The variables I and J are used to select where on the screen to draw the square. In this program we made I and J the center of the screen. Finally the HPLOT statement in line 60 draws the actual square, using I and J as the "reference" points, and X and Y as the sides of the square.

Example 12:

Write a program to draw four boxes of various sizes on the Apple II in high-resolution color. Use DATA statements to hold the corner coordinates of the boxes and let N equal the number of boxes.

Solution:

```
10 HGR: HCOLOR=3: F=1.212
15 N=4                          Number of boxes
20 FOR L=1 TO N
25 READ I,J,XS,YS               Location of box and its dimensions
30 X=XS*F/2: Y=YS/2
35 HPLOT I-X,J-Y TO I+X,J-Y
   TO I+X,J+Y TO I-X,J+Y
   TO I-X,J-Y
40 NEXT L
45 END
100 DATA 140,80,100,100         Each data/statement holds I, J, XS,
105 DATA 140,80,200,15          and YS
110 DATA 50,40,20,20
115 DATA 230,60,5,100
```

See Fig. 3-12.

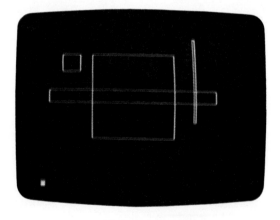

Fig. 3-12. Plot of four boxes.

To make things even more flexible we can use the DATA statement to store the coordinates of the corners of the box. Then we can structure our program so it can display several boxes with each box described by its own DATA statement (we will extend this idea often in the text). See Example 12.

Example 13:

Write a program to draw three right triangles with angles of 30°, 45°, and 80° on the Apple II in hires.

Solution:

```
 10 HGR: HCOLOR=3: F=1.212
 15 PI=3.14159
 20 N=3                          ──── Number of triangles
 25 FOR K=1 TO N
 30 READ I,J,O,T                 ──── Location of 90° corner, length of
 35 T=90−T: T=T/180*PI                opposite side, angle T
 40 A=O/TAN(T)/F                 ──── Finds length of adjacent side
 45 HPLOT I,J TO I−O,J TO O,J−A   Plots a triangle
    TO I,J
 50 NEXT K
 55 END
100 DATA 140,80,70,45
105 DATA 240,120,200,30
110 DATA 50,150,30,80
```

See Fig. 3-13.

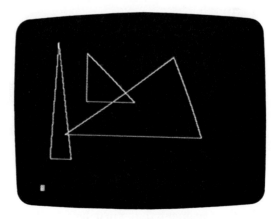

Fig. 3-13. Plot of three right triangles.

The FOR...NEXT loop in statement 20 causes the program to read a DATA statement and assign the values in it to the variables I and J (the location of the box center) and then XS and YS (the length of the sides of the box). Next, in statement 30 we multiply XS by the correction factor F and divide XS and YS by 2 to get the half-side length. Finally, statement 35 is like the previous program statement 60; it plots the box shape according to the variables I, J, X, and Y. The loop then repeats for the next N−1 boxes.

Triangles

Triangles (of the right-angle type) may be generated by specifying a corner location (I,J) for positioning the triangle, an opposite side (O), and an angle (call it T) in the range of 0° to 90°. We can then use the formula

$$A = O/\tan T$$

to find the length of the adjacent side (A) and then divide by F to correct for screen distortion. Since T is specified in degrees we can convert to radians with the formula:

$$T_r = T_d/\ 180\ /\ \pi$$

where π=3.14159. See Example 13, p. 119.

The first two values in the DATA statements are the location of the right-angle (90°) corner, the third value is the length of the opposite side, and the last value is the angle in degrees. Other than that the program is just like the previous one. You can add more triangles by adding more DATA statements and adjusting N.

Regular Polygons

Polygons are those closed figures having three or more sides and each side may be any length. The polygons we are most familiar with are the "regular" polygons, i.e. those with equal-length sides, such as the pentagon, hexagon, and so on.

To draw polygons on a computer with vector graphics is similar to the way we plot circles, except instead of plotting points we draw lines. See Example 14, p. 121.

Some oddities worth mentioning in the program—the FOR ...NEXT loop which generates the angles T is:

```
FOR T=A1 TO A2+.01 STEP INC
```

The +.01 is an increment that must be added to A2 to ensure that the loop doesn't skip the last value of T (6.28313), which can happen due to rounding errors.

Example 14:

Write a program to draw a pentagon (five sides), hexagon (six sides), and an octagon (eight sides) on the Apple II in hires. Use the circle generation approach and make the polygons concentric (all have the same center). Let N = number of sides, L = number of polygons, and R = radius of polygon.

Solution:

```
 10 HGR: HCOLOR=3: PI=3.14159
 15 F=1.212: A1=0: A2=2*PI
 20 L=3
 25 FOR S=1 TO L
 30 READ I,J,R,N
 35 INC=(A2−A1)/N
 40 FOR T=A1 TO A2+.01 STEP INC
 45 X=R*SIN(T)
 50 Y=R*COS(T)/F
 55 IF T=A1 THEN HPLOT I+X,J+Y
 60 HPLOT TO I+X,J+Y
 65 NEXT T: NEXT S
 70 END
100 DATA 140,80,50,5
105 DATA 140,80,60,6
110 DATA 140,80,70,8
```

See Fig. 3-14.

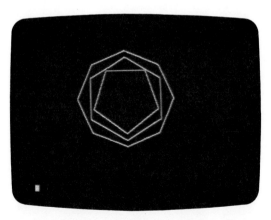

Fig. 3-14. Plot of three concentric polygons.

The variable F adjusts the polygons for screen distortion. The IF...THEN statement at line 55 is needed because of the nature of the HPLOT TO statement, and it locates the first dot location for the later line vectors.

Circles

We can produce a convincing display of the beauties of math by noting that as the number of sides in the polygon increases, the more the polygon resembles a circle (Example 15).

Example 15:

Draw four concentric circles, using the "polygon" approach, starting with 8 sides, then increasing to 10, 15, and finally 45 sides. Have the radius of each circle increase as the number of sides increases so we can see the differences.

Solution:

```
10 HGR: HCOLOR=3: PI=3.14159
15 F=1.212: A1=0: A2=2*PI
20 L=4

      .
{as in previous program}
      .
      .

100 DATA  140,80,30,8
105 DATA  140,80,40,10
110 DATA  140,80,55,15
115 DATA  140,80,75,45
```

See Fig. 3-15.

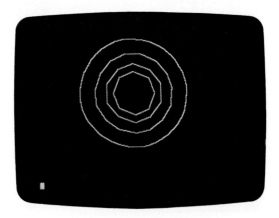

Fig. 3-15. Polygon approach to plotting circles.

Now let's review what we have covered in this section. The concepts for drawing simple geometric shapes have been shown. We have also seen the techniques for making our shapes "relocatable" and for making them change size easily.

In the next section we shall explore concepts for making figures for game programs—figures that can be moved, bounced, or shot across the screen.

GAMING FIGURES

Gaming figures are those figures drawn on a computer screen for playing games. They include such things as balls, tanks, chessmen, and so on. For example, in a PONG game the gaming figure is a ball that the computer makes bounce around on the screen. In a game of tank war the gaming figure is a tank that we can move on the screen with an external control called a "paddle" or "joystick."

Unlike most low-cost graphics computers the Apple II (in hires) has a unique method for handling gaming figures called *shape tables*. But before we cover this unique approach to gaming figures let's see the alternative approach that uses the more mundane features of BASIC and is easier to understand.

Elementary Gaming Figures

The simplest approach to creating a gaming figure (for vector graphics displays, that is) involves the storing of "vector end points" for a figure, inside of DATA statements, reading them into an array, and then using the array elements in a HPLOT statement inside a FOR...NEXT loop.

The actual technique for creating a vector end-point shape is as follows. First you get a piece of 0.1-inch (0.25-cm) grid paper (blue grid is best). Then draw the desired shape on the grid using lines and a "connect-the-dot" strategy, that is, outlining the shape with as few points as possible and then connecting these points with straight lines. Next you draw an imaginary X axis and Y axis through the middle of the shape. Then you read off the X and Y coordinates for each point, moving in a clockwise direction through the shape, while making a list. The values in the list are then placed in DATA statements in a BASIC program. The program reads the values into an array and then uses these values to draw the shape on the screen. Once we have the values for the end points of the shape in an array we can do all kinds of tricky things using the math functions of BASIC, including shrinking, translation, expanding, rotation, and so on.

Let's look at Example 15, showing how easy this is.

Example 16:

Draw a bird shape on ⅒-inch grid paper using a "connect-the-dot" strategy. Use as few dots as possible. Draw a vertical and horizontal axis through the middle of the shape; then make up a list of the X and Y values for each point on the shape.

Solution:

See Fig. 3-16.

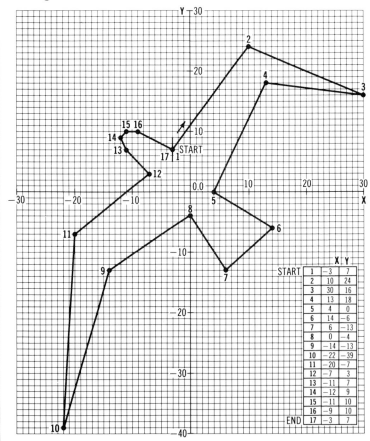

Fig. 3-16. Drawing a bird using 17 points on a grid.

	X	Y
START 1	−3	7
2	10	24
3	30	16
4	13	18
5	4	0
6	14	−6
7	6	−13
8	0	−4
9	−14	−13
10	−22	−39
11	−20	−7
12	−7	3
13	−11	7
14	−12	9
15	−11	10
16	−9	10
END 17	−3	7

As you can see in Fig. 3-16 a list has been made of the co-ordinates of the X and Y points starting with point 1 at $(-3,7)$ and ending with point 17. Since the shape has only 17 points it won't take long to draw on the screen. The next step is to write a program to use the list of end points (Example 17).

Example 17:

Write a program for drawing the previous shape using the values in the list of Fig. 3-16. Store all the points in an array $X(I)$ and $Y(I)$ and then have the program draw lines between these points.

Solution:

```
10 HGR: HCOLOR=3: F=1.212
15 N=16: DIM X(N), Y(N)          ─┤Dimensions arrays X(I) and Y(I)
20 FOR I=0 TO N: READ X(I): NEXT I │ that will hold coordinates of
25 FOR I=0 TO N: READ Y(I):        │ gaming figure
   Y(I)=-Y(I)/F: NEXT I          ─►Fill arrays from data statements
30 HPLOT 140+X(0),80+Y(0)
35 FOR I=1 TO N                  ─┤Begin loop that draws the gam-
40 HPLOT TO 140+X(I),80+Y(I)       │ ing figure
45 NEXT I
50 END
10000 DATA -3,10,30,13,4,14,6,0,-14,-22,─Coordinates for gaming figure
      -20,-7,-11,-12,-11,-9,-3
20000 DATA 7,24,16,18,0,-6,-13,-4,-13,
      -39,-7,3,7,9,10,10,7
```

See Fig. 3-17.

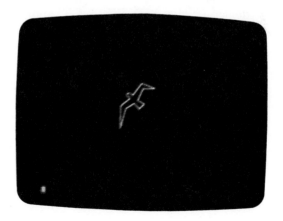

Fig. 3-17. Computer plot of bird of Fig. 3-16.

As you can see in Fig. 3-17, the bird shape is drawn almost exactly like it looks on the paper, except it is smaller. The program starts by switching into the high-resolution graphics mode in statement 10, then it sets N to equal the number of end points in the list minus 1 and DIMensions two arrays X(N) and Y(N). Next, in statement 20 we read in the elements of the X(I) array from the first DATA statement (statement 10000). Statement 25 is similar and reads in the Y(I) elements from DATA statement 20000. It also flips the Y(I) values upside down to compensate for the reversed Y axis of the Apple, and divides the Y(I) elements by F to compensate for the Y axis screen distortion.

In statement 30 we do an initial HPLOT using X(0) and Y(0) to get the first point on the screen. Next, in statement 35 we enter a FOR...NEXT loop that uses each element of X(I) and Y(I) in an HPLOT TO statement to draw the bird on the screen. Note the drawing loop starts with element 1 of each array because we used element 0 to define the starting point.

That is all there is to it, except, of course, the problem of moving the shape on the screen and changing its relative size. Let's look at both of these problems.

Moving the Shape

To move a shape which is defined by vector end points in an array we simply play with the values of the constants in the HPLOT TO statement that are added to the vector elements. Suppose, for example, we wanted the bird shape to appear to fly across the screen automatically. See Example 18, p. 127.

As you can see, the complexity of our program is growing, but the program becomes easier to understand. The first GOSUB 1000 statement causes the X and Y arrays to be filled with the information in the DATA statements. The variable P is used later to set the STEP size of a FOR...NEXT loop which controls the velocity of the movement (big steps make it move faster compared to small steps). The variable J is used to set the vertical position for the bird to a constant, such as 80 here.

At statement 40 we enter the main drawing loop, in which the variable I goes from 240 to 25 stepping by −15 to begin. We set the HCOLOR to white and then GOSUB to line 100, which causes the shape to be drawn out at location I,J on the screen.

Next, we change HCOLOR to black and erase the shape that is on the screen now. The loop is incremented and the process repeats until the shape reaches the left side of the screen, whereupon we make P larger and repeat the loop again. Since the step size is larger now the shape will appear to move faster.

That's all there is to it!

Shape Table Gaming Figures

Although the previous method for creating gaming figures (using floating-point arrays and DATA statements) is flexible and easy to visualize, it suffers from these problems:

1. Speed—Floating-point BASIC array operations are just too slow for fast-acting animation. Therefore forget about using them for PONG games. They do work, however, for games where slow movement is permissible.
2. No "Undraw"—There is no easy way to erase a shape without also erasing the drawing information underneath it. For example, if you have a green grid drawn on a black background and you draw a violet bird on the grid, when you erase the bird by drawing it in black you will wipe out a portion of the green grid.
3. Hard to rotate, expand, etc.—Complex transformations often involving BASIC trig functions are required when you wish to rotate or expand a shape. These transformations are very slow and make fast-action animation impossible.

Anticipating that graphics users would want some powerful software for dealing with gaming figures, the designer of the Apple II cleverly incorporated the concept of *shape tables* in Applesoft, the floating-point BASIC.

A shape table is created by outlining a shape with tiny unit vectors which are all the same length but may be any one of four directions (up, down, left, right). The vectors are placed head to tail until the shape is outlined. Next, using a simple

---

Example 18:

Change the previous bird drawing program to cause the bird to move from the right side to the screen to the left, so it looks like the bird is flying. Also, see if you can make the speed of the bird increase each time it sweeps across the screen. Two main tips are:
1. Change the HPLOT TO 140+X(I),80+Y(I) statement to HPLOT TO I+X(I),J+Y(I). The variable I controls the horizontal position and the variable J controls the vertical movement.
2. Make the drawing part of the previous program a subroutine and make the main program a FOR...NEXT loop that increments the horizontal variable I, erases the old bird, and then draws the new bird in its new position.

Solution:

```
  10 HGR: HCOLOR=3: F=1.212
  20 GOSUB 1000 ————————————————— Fill array subroutine
  30 P=15: J=80 ————————————————┐P is the velocity, J the verti-
  40 FOR I=240 TO 25 STEP —P ◄── │   cal position
  45 HCOLOR=3:GOSUB 100          └ Main draw and erase loop
  50 FOR D=1 TO 50: NEXT D          Draw it
  55 HCOLOR=0: GOSUB 100            Erase it
  60 NEXT I
  65 P=P+2 ◄————————————————————— Increase velocity
  70 GOTO 40
 100 HPLOT I+X(0),J+Y(0): FOR K=1 TO N:◄─┐Draw gaming figure
     HPLOT TO I+X(K),J+Y(K): NEXT K:     │ subroutine
     RETURN
1000 N=16: DIM X(N), Y(N) ◄────────────┐Subroutine to fill gaming
1010 FOR I=0 TO N: READ X(I): NEXT I:   │ figure array with coordi-
     FOR I=0 TO N: READ Y(I):           │ nates
     Y(I) = —Y(I)/F: NEXT I:
     RETURN
10000 DATA —3,10,30,13,4,14,6,0,—14,—22,
           —20,—7,—11,—12,—11,—9,—3
20000 DATA 7,24,16,18,0,—6,—13,—4,—13,
           —39,—7,3,7,9,10,10,7
```

See Fig. 3-18.

Fig. 3-18. Moving computer plot of bird.

key, these direction vectors are converted to a string of bytes and then stored in memory as part of a shape table.

You can store up to 255 shapes in a single table in memory. Once you have the object represented in a shape table you can get BASIC to draw it anywhere on the screen with the statement:

DRAW 1 AT X,Y

and you can erase the shape without erasing what is underneath it (nondestructive erase) with the statement:

XDRAW 1 AT X,Y

Here the 1 represents shape number 1 in the shape table and X,Y is any location on the screen.

Now the really great thing about these shapes is that you can have BASIC rotate the shape through 360° with the statement:

ROT=0–64

The value after ROT sets one of 65 angles for the shape to be in when DRAW is used.

You can change the size of the shape from very small to larger than the screen with the statement:

SCALE=1–255

The value after SCALE selects a size for all the unit vectors between 1 and 255. With SCALE you can make your shape expand or shrink on the screen in less than an eyeblink.

After you have constructed a shape with the vectors and the key conversion, you can save it permanently on cassette tape and then read it back into your BASIC program with the statement:

SHLOAD

which stands for SHape LOAD. Actually SHLOAD loads an entire shape table with up to 255 shapes in it.

Making a Shape Using a Shape Table

The actual procedure for creating a shape for a shape table is fairly simple but rather time-consuming. For this reason we will only cover the construction of a very simple shape with few vectors. We will, however, use more complex shapes in some later demonstrations in the book. See Example 19.

Example 19:

Show the steps for creating a shape table for a simple gaming figure, such as a Star Wars Tie Fighter™.

Solution:

The seven steps to creating a gaming figure for a shape table are design the shape out of vectors, unwrap the vectors, convert the unwrapped vectors to a table of hex bytes, add a header to the table, load the table into memory, save the table on tape, and finally load the table on tape into a BASIC program. Here is the complete procedure for a simple Tie Fighter gaming figure.

Step 1.   Design the Shape

In Fig. 3-19A 0.1-inch (0.25-cm) grid paper was used to draw the outline of the gaming figure. To make the image on the screen look like the picture we draw on paper, we make the vertical vectors 0.3 inch (0.75 cm) and the horizontal vectors 0.4 inch or 1.0 cm (this makes the horizontal vectors 25 percent longer than the vertical vectors). The first vector starts at the approximate center of the shape so that when the shape is rotated the first vector spins about its center. The first vector is shown dashed to indicate that it is a move without actually plotting, i.e., we move but there is no vector drawn on the screen. Follow the vectors around the shape clockwise. The shape has 33 vectors when it is completed.

Step 2.   Unwrap the Vectors

Unwrap the vectors left to right, starting with vector 1 (see Fig. 3-19B).

Step 3.   Convert Vectors to Hex

Using the key shown in Fig. 3-19C, convert the vectors into a table of binary bytes and then convert these to hex values. Note the way the vectors are entered into the table. Section A is filled first, then B, then C, and then we move to section A of the next byte, i.e., the vectors are stored in right-to-left format.

Step 4.   Add the Header

Since up to 255 shapes can be placed in a single shape table a header must be added to indicate how many shapes are stored and where the first shape begins. In the Apple this header indicates there is one shape and it starts four bytes from the table beginning. (See Fig. 3-19D.) We also must add a zero byte to the end of the shape to indicate the end of the shape.

Step 5.   Load the Table into Memory

(a)   Find the total table length. Here it is 22 bytes. Convert this to hex. Here this is hex 16. Load this number into memory locations 00 and 01 from the monitor

   *0:16 00

(b)   Load the table into memory from the monitor using a memory area that is temporarily free and won't be clobbered from BASIC easily. If your table is less than 255 bytes use locations 300 to 3FF in the Apple. If your table is really long then you can

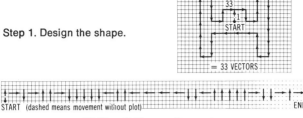

(A) Step 1. Design the shape.

= 33 VECTORS

START (dashed means movement without plot) END

(B) Step 2. Unwrap the vectors.

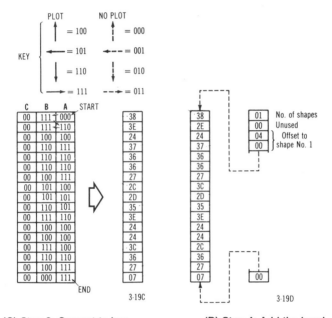

(C) Step 3: Convert to hex. (D) Step 4: Add the head.

Fig. 3-19. Creating shape table figure.

set aside a high area of memory that BASIC won't touch for the table. But if you have a 16K machine you must make the table be below 8192. The author uses locations 1D00 to 1FFF and sets HIMEM to 7424. This frees 768 bytes for shapes, which is about 1400–2100 vectors. Enter the table (from Fig. 3-19D) using the Apple monitor.

*1D00:01 00 04 ....25 05 00

You may wish to fill your shape table area with zeros (0's) before you load in the actual shape bytes. This will make it easier to examine the table from the monitor once its loaded in from tape. You can even put the zeros on the tape if you change the range of the tape write and read commands.

Step 6.   Store the Table on Tape

Save the current table in memory to cassette tape so it can be later called up with SHLOAD. Use the monitor to write the table like this:

    *0.1W 1D00.1D16W

The 0.1W writes the standard Apple header to the tape (table length in two bytes). The 1D00.1D16W writes the actual shape table data on the tape.

   You should understand that at this point the shape will be saved on tape, and when SHLOAD is used next to load the table we can forget about where it is and how long it is.

Step 7.   Load the Shape into Basic

To load the shape table stored on tape into a BASIC program we get into BASIC, start the recorder at the beginning of the table, and type:

    SHLOAD

(You may also need to type HIMEM:8192 if you have a 16K Apple.)

If you have a disk based Apple you will want to skip steps 6 and 7 and save the table on disk as follows:

Step 8. Get back into DOS without bombing the table you have entered from the monitor. Use control-C to do this. Now use BSAVE to save the table onto the disk:

    BSAVE TIEFIGHT, A$1D00, L$20

   Here TIEFIGHT is the name we choose for the name of the shape table (any other will do), A$1D00 is the hex start address of the table and L$20 is the hex length of the table. We used hex 20 instead of 16 to get some extra zeros on the end of the file.

Step 9. To have your BASIC demo program automatically load the shape table off the disk when its RUN, add the following statement to your program:

    1000 PRINT " DBLOAD, A$1D00, L$20"

   You can remove the old statements 1000-1030 since you will find loading from disk is almost as fast as loading from RAM. The D in the above means type control and the D key together. This tells the Apple the following statement is a DOS command (which BSAVE and BLOAD are).

Paddle Control of Shape Position

   One of the most interesting uses of gaming figures is in games where joysticks or paddles are used to move the shape about on the screen. High-resolution shapes are made for this, as we will see in the next program example (Example 20).

   The program starts out by switching into the graphics mode and setting the HCOLOR to white. Next we set the SCALE to be 5 and the ROTation to 0.

Example 20:

Assuming the previous shape or one like it has been loaded into memory with SHLOAD, design a program that allows you to move the shape table gaming figure anywhere on the screen using a paddle or a joystick. Use the DRAW statements and set the SCALE to 5 and the ROTation to 0.

Solution:

```
  5 MAX=25 ————————————————— Sets length of draw delay time
 10 HGR: HCOLOR=3
 20 ROT=0: SCALE=5
100 X=PDL(0): Y=PDL(1)/1.6 ——— Read the paddle positions
110 DRAW 1 AT X,Y ——————————— Draw the shape
120 FOR I=1 TO MAX: NEXT I ——— Delay for an instant
130 XDRAW 1 AT X,Y ——————————— Un-draw the shape
140 GOTO 100 ————————————————— Repeat entire process
```

See Fig. 3-20.

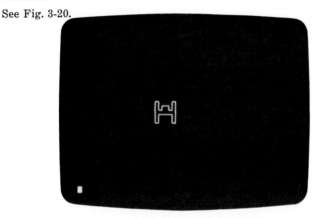

Fig. 3-20. Plot of Tie Fighter shape.

In line 100 we measure paddle PDL(0) to get a value between 0 and 255 for the X position. On the same line we measure paddle PDL(1) and divide it by 1.6 to get a value between 0 and 159 for the Y position. Recall that we have already loaded the shape with SHLOAD and it is sitting in memory waiting to be drawn on the screen.

Statement 110 draws the shape in the table on the screen at position X,Y. Then a delay occurs by the FOR...NEXT loop in statement 120. This is necessary because the DRAW and XDRAW statements are so fast that flickering will occur unless we hold the shape on the screen for a brief fraction of a second.

Finally, in statement 130 we undraw and erase the shape with XDRAW, and in statement 140 we GOTO line 100 to repeat this draw and undraw process as a loop.

This program clearly demonstrates how easy it is to shuttle shapes across the screen. They move fast and smoothly. There are none of the problems of lag.

Paddle Control of SCALE and ROTation

Now to see how the SCALE and ROT statements work we can fix the X,Y position and use the paddles to control the scale and rotation. See Example 21.

Example 21:

Add to the previous program so that we can control the SCALE and the ROTation with the two paddles or a joystick.

Solution:

```
200 HGR: HCOLOR=3
205 X=140: Y=80: MAX=25 ←————————— Fix the X,Y position
210 ROT=PDL(0)/4: SCALE=PDL(1)/8+1 ←| Set rotation and scale according
220 DRAW 1 AT X,Y                    |   to paddles or joystick
230 FOR I=1 TO MAX: NEXT I
240 XDRAW 1 AT X,Y
250 GOTO 200
```

See Fig. 3-21.

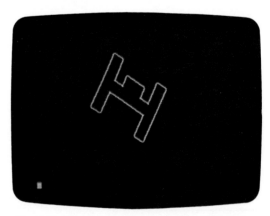

Fig. 3-21. Altering scale and rotation of Tie Fighter.

The most important thing in the program is to restrict the range of ROT to 0 to 64 (see line 210). The range of SCALE is kept between 1 and 64 to keep the shape from being larger than the screen (which would cause the shape to wrap around the screen).

Black Shapes on White Backgrounds

To make a simple change in the program that has a major effect on the display try reversing the color of the shape from white to black. See Example 22.

Example 22:

Show the simple but slow brute-force approach to generating a white background, and for contrast the fast slick CALL subroutine for changing screen color in a flash.

Solution:

The slow way:
```
300 HGR: HCOLOR=3
310 FOR Y=0 TO 159
320 HPLOT 0,Y TO 279,Y
330 NEXT Y
340 HCOLOR=0: GOTO 205
```
The fast way:
```
400 HGR: HCOLOR=3: HPLOT 0,0:
    CALL 62454◄───────────────────  This is a neat machine language subrou-
410 HCOLOR=0: GOTO 205              tine in Applesoft that fills screen with
                                    last HCOLOR
```

The second method uses a CALL statement to almost instantaneously switch the screen color. The color is the last HCOLOR executed in the program. An HPLOT statement must be executed before the CALL statement is issued.

MANDALAS AND COMPUTER ART

The new graphic computer presents unlimited possibilities for the programmer interested in art or the artist interested in programming. What is really appealing about computer art type programs is that they are usually short and sweet, re-

Example 23:

Create a "rotating fan" demonstration program using high-resolution graphics on the Apple. Make the fan rotate around the screen and have it change color on a random basis.

Solution:

```
 15 GOTO 600
 60 HPLOT 279-X,191-Y TO X,Y          Draw a line
 61 J=J+1: IF J>CNT THEN J=0:         After a random number of J iterations,
    CNT=RND(1)*50: HPLOT 0,0:          a new CNT value is created and
    HCOLOR=RND(1)*7                    a new color is selected
 62 RETURN                            POKE  -16302,0 removes
600 REM ROTATING FAN                  scrolling text window
605 HGR: POKE -16302,0: HCOLOR=3:     First fan is white
    CNT=25: X=0: Y=0: J=0
610 FOR X=1 TO 278
615 GOSUB 60: NEXT X
620 FOR Y=1 TO 190
625 GOSUB 60: NEXT Y
630 FOR X=278 TO 1 STEP -1
635 GOSUB 60: NEXT X
640 FOR Y=192 TO 1 STEP -1
645 GOSUB 60: NEXT Y
650 GOTO 610
```

See Fig. 3-22.

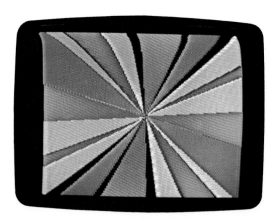

Fig. 3-22. Plot of "rotating fan" with changing colors.

quiring a minimum amount of time to create. Of course, you can get quite elaborate, but this is true for any program.

In this section we will see how the computer can be used to create far-out fantasy special effects, from simple mandala-like displays to complex "tunneling" demonstration programs using shape tables.

Simple Vector Graphics Art

For simple graphics programs we can use the HPLOT TO and HCOLOR statements. The main thing to keep in mind when writing a graphics program is: "How fast does it run?" If a graphics program is too slow in executing, then in general it will also be too boring for people to watch for long. So let's take a look at two simple graphics programs that use the HPLOT TO and HCOLOR= statements. See Example 23.

The line numbers in the program are 600 because we are saving line 100–599 for later demonstrations. Until otherwise mentioned a demonstration module uses line numbers 100–199, 200–299, ... ,900–999. This allows for nine demonstration segments in a program.

The program is built around four FOR...NEXT loops in lines 100 to 140. The purpose of the loops is to make the values of X and Y vary as if we are following a path around the perimeter of the screen. This is accomplished by the indexes of the FOR...NEXT loops. The subroutine in line 50 does an HPLOT TO from the X,Y point on the screen edge to the exact opposite side. The subroutine then increments a variable J, compares it to the variable CNT, and, if it's larger, resets J to zero, chooses a new random color and a new value for CNT, and RETURNS. If the variable J is not larger than CNT the program simply returns to draw the next line of the fan.

You can exploit the technique behind this demonstration program to make other mandala type effects. The main idea is to make variables count up so as to represent some path around the screen edge, and then do an HPLOT TO to draw a line related to the path. See Example 24, p. 138.

This program uses the technique of storing point pairs in arrays. The resulting display appears to spiral toward a point. The equations in statements 760–765 shrink the size of the values in the arrays while shifting them slightly in one direction. Then the points are connected by the HPLOT TO statement in line 755.

Graphics Art With Shape Tables

What about artistic demonstrations using shape tables? It turns out that some incredible visual effects can be created using the shape table feature of the Apple. What is special

Example 24:

Create an artistic demonstration called "slinky" in which a point is projected into a random corner on the Apple. HINT: Fill an array with random X,Y pairs. Use the values in a simple equation that makes the set of points grow smaller. Connect the points with an HPLOT TO statement.

Solution:

```
  15 GOTO 700
 700 REM SLINKY
 705 CLEAR: DIM X(10), Y(10) ◄——— CLEAR makes all variables zero
 710 HOME: HGR: POKE −16302,0 ◄——┤ HOME clears the screen and puts cur-
 715 C=INT(RND(1)*7+1): ◄—         │ sor at top left corner of screen
     IF C=0 OR C=4 THEN C=2        │ Generates a random number for setting
 720 HCOLOR=C                      │ color
 725 R=RND(1)*7+1
 730 FOR I=1 TO R: ◄——————————————— Fill array with random points
     X(I)=RND(1)*279:
     Y(I)=RND(1)*191:
     NEXT I
 735 REM
 740 X=RND(1)*279: Y=RND(1)*191
 745 HPLOT X,Y ◄——————————————————— Locate beginning coordinate
 750 FOR J=1 TO 30: FOR I=1 TO R ◄— Begin draw loop
 755 HPLOT TO X(I), Y(I) ◄————————— Draw line between points
 760 X(I)=(X(I)−X)*.9+X ◄——
 765 Y(I)=(Y(I)−Y)*.9+Y ◄——————————— Shrink and shift values in array
 770 NEXT I: NEXT J
 775 GOTO 710
```

See Fig. 3-23.

Fig. 3-23. Projecting a point into a random corner.

about these demonstrations is that they are very fast and amazingly simple. Let's take a look at Example 25.

Example 25:

Design a simple demonstration program that uses shapes. Store two simple shapes, a square and a cross, in a table. Write one demonstration that simply changes the scale and draws the shape over. Write another that changes scale and rotation together to cause a tunneling effect. Have a menu that allows the user to select a demonstration. Have the program alternate between the two shapes.

Solution:

Design the Shape Table

The first step is to design the shape table. Instead of using SHLOAD and storing our shape on tape we will store it in a DATA statement and have the program POKE it in at the beginning.

Fig. 3-24 is the layout for the shapes and the conversions to the proper hex bytes.

Next we create a little program that stores the bytes in a DATA statement and loads the values into memory when executed. The pro-

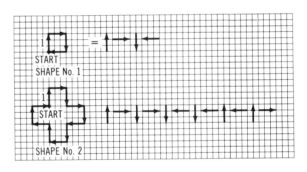

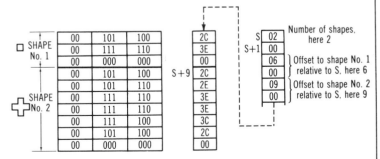

Fig. 3-24. Shape table details for computer art demonstration.

gram also POKEs in the starting address of the shape table (this is
necessary for the Apple when you don't use SHLOAD).

```
1000 REM LOADS THE TABLE START ADDRESS
1005 POKE 232,0: POKE 233,3 ◄──────────┤232=low byte, 233=high byte,
1006 RESTORE                           │ here address is 300 hex
1010 REM LOAD THE ACTUAL TABLE  ┐Shape table decimal beginning
1015 FOR LOC=768 TO 783 ◄────────┘  & end
1020 READ BYTE: POKE LOC,BYTE   ┌─Derived from table in Fig. 3-24
1025 NEXT LOC                   └
1030 DATA 2,0,6,0,9,0,44,62,0,44,46,62,62,60,44,0 ◄──┘
```

Menu

New before we write the actual demonstration modules a menu is
needed to allow the user to select a program. Here is the menu and
the beginning parts of program:

```
   0 GOTO 1000
  50 C=INT(RND(1)*6+1): HCOLOR=C: ◄─Random color generation
     IF C=4 THEN HCOLOR=3
  55 RETURN                         Change line 650 to GOTO 0,
 600–650 previous Fan program ──── change line 775 to GOTO 0, re-
 700–775 previous Slinky program   move line 15.
1000 REM LOADS THE SHAPE TABLE START ADDRESS
1005 POKE 232,0: POKE 233,3
1010 REM LOADS THE ACTUAL TABLE DATA
1015 FOR LOC=768 TO 783
1020 READ BYTE: POKE LOC,BYTE
1025 NEXT LOC
1030 DATA 2,0,6,0,9,0,44,62,0,44,46,62,62,60,44,0
1200 M=60: M1=1: MAX=15: ROT=0:
     SCALE=5: X=140: Y=95: CNT=25
2000 REM MENU STARTS HERE
2001 HOME: VTAB 21
2005 PRINT "1 EXPLODE   2 VORTEX   3 SNOWFLAKE"
2010 PRINT "4 FALLING   5 FLASHER   6 FAN"
2015 PRINT "7 SLINKY"
2020 PRINT "SELECTION? ";
2021 POKE −16301 ,0: GET S ◄───────┤GET returns the key pressed in
2025 IF S<1 OR S>7 THEN 2015        │ variable S
2030 K=NOT K: SH=K+1 ◄──────────────┤Switches shape (SH) between
2035 IF SH=2 THEN M=60              │ square and cross
2040 IF SH=1 THEN M=80
2045 ON S GOTO 100,200,300,400,500,600,700
```

Note that we loaded the shape data into decimal address 768 to 783.
This region (300 to 3FF hex) in memory is free to the Apple user
for machine language programs and it is not written over by any
monitor or system commands.

The subroutine in line 50 is for selecting a color for the background
for some of the demonstrations.

The menu is set up for easy expansion by using the ON...GOTO
statement. As you can see in the menu there is room for our original
programs (fan and slinky projection into corner) as well as some
new demonstrations we will now investigate.

Demonstration No. 1.   Explode

The first demonstration, Explode, is very simple. Enter it into the previous program:

```
100 REM EXPLODE
105 HGR: POKE −16302,0: X=140: Y=95
110 FOR M1=1 TO MAX
115 HCOLOR=0: HPLOT 0,0: CALL 62454:
    GOSUB 50: ROT=RND(1)*64 ←————————— Random rotation set
120 FOR I=1 TO M STEP M1
125 SCALE=I ←————————————————————— Scale grows larger
130 DRAW SH AT X,Y ←———————————————— Draw shape (SH) at X,Y
135 NEXT I,M1
140 GOTO 0 ←——————————————————————— Return to menu
```

See Fig. 3-25.

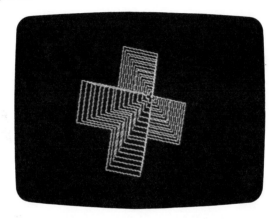

Fig. 3-25. "Explode" demonstration.

When this program is executed (by selecting 1 on the menu) it clears the screen to black. The POKE-16302,0 statement removes the scrolling window at the bottom of the screen so that the screen extends vertically to 193. The "M1" FOR...NEXT loop is used to generate STEP values of 1 to 15. Statement 115 clears the screen to black with the fast CALL statement. The GOSUB 50 chooses a random HCOLOR for the shape. The ROTation is set to a random value between 0 and 64. In line 120 we enter the main loop of the program. Here the SCALE is set to the value of I, and the statement DRAW SH AT X,Y draws shape SH (SH=1 or 2) at position 140,95 on the screen. Then the SCALE is expanded and we draw the shape again and this is repeated M times. The STEP size keeps increasing, so the shape appears to be drawn faster each time. The result is like an explosion. After 15 of these explosions statement 140 sends us to statement 0, which clears the screen, re-establishes the scrolling window, and sends us back to the menu.

Demonstration No. 2.   Vortex

The next demonstration is called *Vortex*. It is like the previous program except: (1) rotation and scale are changed each time the shape is drawn so that it twists as it expands and (2) the background is made to be a color (green or violet) rather than black, and the shape's HCOLOR is made black.

```
200 REM VORTEX
205 HGR: POKE −16302,0: X=140: Y=95
210 GOSUB 50: HPLOT 0,0: CALL 62454
215 L=NOT L: HCOLOR=L*4: IF L THEN 230
220 FOR I=1 TO M ───────────────── Expanding shape loop
225 GOTO 235
230 FOR I=M TO 1 STEP −1 ───────── Contracting shape loop
235 ROT=I: SCALE=I ──────────────── Change scale and rotation to I
240 DRAW SH AT X,Y ──────────────── Draw the shape
245 NEXT I
250 J=J+1: IF J=6 THEN J=0: GOTO 0 ──┤ Repeat demo 6 times and then
255 GOTO 210                          │ return to menu
```

See Fig. 3-26.

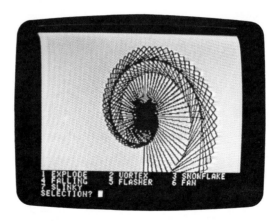

Fig. 3-26. "Vortex" demonstration.

In this program we use the variable L for two things. L is made to alternate between the values 0 and 1 by the statement L=NOT L. This way L can be used to switch the color between the two blacks on Apple (The black=0 color goes with violet and green colors while the black=4 goes with blue and orange. The blue and orange colors are available on the new Apples.) Switching the black like this gives an unusual effect when the wrong black is used with a color (such as black=0 on a blue background). The other use for L is to make the vortex either expand outward or contract inward. This is accomplished by using L to choose which FOR...NEXT loop will be used. One loop increments I in the direction opposite to the other.

At the end of the program, line 250 increments J and compares it to 6 to see if it's time to end the VORTEX demonstration.

Demonstration No. 3.   Snowflake

Here is a simple variation of the previous program that changes the scale of the shape in steps of 7 instead of 1. The shape is rotated through 360° before the next scale is used. What this does is result in a spinning display that alternates between growing outward or inward.

```
300 REM SNOWFLAKE
305 HGR: POKE −16302,0
310 HCOLOR=0: HPLOT 0,0: CALL 62454
315 L=NOT L: IF L THEN 330
320 FOR H=5 TO 50 STEP 7
325 GOTO 335
330 FOR H=50 TO 5 STEP −1          Subroutine at 50 generates a
335 SCALE=H: GOSUB 50              random color
340 FOR I=1 TO M STEP RND(1)*6+2   Step is made random 2-8
345 ROT=I
350 DRAW SH AT X,Y
355 NEXT I,H: FOR D=1 TO 1000:
    NEXT D
360 J=J+1: IF J>4 THEN J=0: GOTO 0
365 GOTO 310
```

See Fig. 3-27.

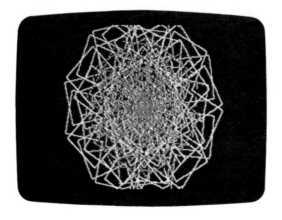

Fig. 3-27. "Snowflake" demonstration.

Demonstration No. 4.   Falling

This demonstration is another variation of EXPLODE, except it changes the values of X and Y so that the shape expands equally in all directions. This gives a visual experience similar to falling down an elevator shaft.

```
400 REM FALLING
406 HGR: POKE −16302,0
410 HCOLOR=0: HPLOT 0,0: CALL 62454
415 M1=RND(1)*3+1: X=140: Y=95
420 FOR I=1 TO M STEP M1
425 SCALE=I
430 DRAW SH AT X,Y
435 X=X+1: Y=Y+1: IF X>278 OR Y>191
    THEN X=140: Y=95: GOTO 445
440 NEXT I
445 J=J+1: IF J>6 THEN J=0: GOTO 0
450 GOTO 410
```

See Fig. 3-28.

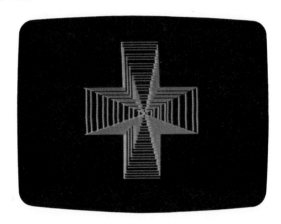

Fig. 3-28. "Falling" demonstration.

Demonstration No. 5   Flasher

The author won't give you any hints on this one. Suffice it to say that no one opens a coat at any time.

```
500 REM FLASHER
505 HGR: POKE −16302,0
510 HCOLOR=RND(1)*6+1: HPLOT 0,0: CALL 62454
515 J=J+1: IF J>20 THEN J=0: GOTO 0
520 GOTO 510
```

Demonstrations Nos. 6 and 7.   Fan and Slinky

The remaining demonstrations (6 and 7) are already installed in the program. Modify the end of each so it returns logically to the calling menu (add the J=J+1 counter).

Using the ideas covered here you can design your own artistic demonstration programs. Because this is such a virgin area, there are still hundreds of effects to be pioneered.

WRITING PONG GAMES IN BASIC

One of the most popular uses for color graphic animation today is for "Pong*"-like computer games. Probably everyone has seen a Pong game before. In fact, last year over 2 million tv games that featured Pong-like action were sold. In a game of Pong, a moving spot, or "ball," glides and rebounds inside a fixed playing field, occasionally striking objects, such as "bricks," and often one or more user-controlled bars, called "paddles." The object of this game is usually to accumulate points, either within a specified time, or to a given limit. There can be one to four players, all playing separately, or competing against each other.

The floating-point BASIC of the Apple is especially suited for writing Pong-like games. The shape tables allow the ball to be any object you wish—a football, frisbee, or golfball, while the paddles can be tennis rackets, baseball bats, or putters. With the rotation commands we can make the ball spin in flight, and with the scale commands we can make it grow larger or shrink while gliding across the screen.

In this section we will explore how to program the Apple to play these games.

The Playfield

The main action of the game takes place on the *playfield,* which on the Apple in the high-resolution mode is a 280 by 160 matrix of colored dots, with a four-line text scrolling window immediately below the graphics matrix. Each dot in the matrix can be one of three colors (white, green, or violet) or can be black.

There are four basic parts to a playfield: the background, the paddle(s), the ball, and (sometimes) several rows or patterns of bricks. There can also be sidewalls bordering the playfield.

To begin the Pong game the HGR statement is used to switch the computer into the high-resolution graphics mode and clear the screen to all black. The scrolling window at the bottom four lines is used for displaying scoring information.

---

* PONG is a registered trademark of Atari, Inc.

Now the background must be drawn. If the color of the background is to be black, then this step can be skipped. If, however, it is to be another color, then these statements should be executed:

```
HCOLOR=C: HPLOT 0,0: CALL 62454
```

assuming C is the desired background color. This fills the entire playfield with color C by using an internal high-resolution assembly routine.

Balls

The major part of any Pong-like game is the ball, usually a moving spot which reflects, rebounds, and oscillates around and through the playfield. In the high-resolution mode we could make the ball a single tiny dot, but it would be very difficult to see as it moved. A better approach is to use a shape table to hold a figure that represents the ball. In this example we could use the shapes presented earlier in the mandala computer art programs, which consist of a square and a simple cross shape. By using two shapes we could have the program switch balls in midgame.

The first thing then is to POKE the game ball shapes into memory as we did in the mandala demonstration program:

```
   1 HIMEM:8046
   2 GOTO 1000
1000 REM LOADS THE TABLE START ADDRESS
1005 POKE 232,0: POKE 233,31: REM (8046)
1010 REM LOAD THE ACTUAL TABLE DATA
1015 FOR LOC=8046 TO 8061: READ BYTE:
     POKE LOC,BYTE: NEXT LOC: GOTO 10
1050 DATA 2,0,6,0,9,0,44,62,0,44,46,62,62,
     60,44,0
```

The basic action involved in moving a ball across the playfield is called an *update loop*. In flowchart form a typical update loop looks like that in Fig. 3-29.

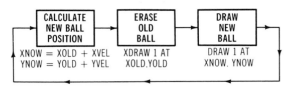

Fig. 3-29. Update loop.

Drawing and erasing the ball in the high-resolution graphics mode are accomplished by use of the DRAW and XDRAW statements. DRAW 1 AT X,Y will draw the ball shape (or any shape defined as shape number 1) at the location specified by the ordered pair (X,Y). XDRAW 1 AT X,Y will erase the same ball, without erasing any object underneath it. This means you can have the ball pass "over" objects in the play-field without erasing them.

Each time the program runs through the update loop it must calculate the new values for XNOW and YNOW (the new location of the ball). This is called "updating," and is accomplished by adding a pair of "velocities" to the old X and old Y values. The velocities determine the angle and the speed of the moving ball. The X velocity determines the speed with which the ball moves back and forth, while the Y velocity determines the vertical deflection speed with respect to the X axis. If the Y velocity is zero, then the ball moves in a straight horizontal line; if the X velocity is zero, then the ball will move directly up and down. The sign (+ or −) of the velocity determines the direction of travel (− for up or left, + for down or right) while the magnitude (absolute value) determines the speed.

Velocities and Angles

Considering the previous ideas, it should be apparent that to move the ball at a shallow angle, the X velocity must be larger than the Y velocity (larger in magnitude, not sign). The reason for this is if the X and Y velocities are equal the ball will move at approximately 45°. Increase the Y velocity and the angle is larger; increase the X velocity and the angle is reduced. The actual angle of travel is a function of the Y velocity divided by the X velocity.

Obviously a Pong game would not be very much fun with only angles of 45° and greater; nor would it be too entertaining if the X velocity was always above 10 (20 is considered fast). Moreover, in Applesoft floating-point BASIC if the X velocity is much less than 1, the ball will move much too slowly. So we will make the game to use velocities between 1 and 20 maximum.

Programming the Update Loop

Due to the nature of most BASIC interpreters, the speed of the update loop is a function of its physical location in the body of the program. If the "draw new ball" step in the flow-chart loops back to "calculate new ball location" by using a

GOTO statement then the BASIC interpreter (particularly in the case of Microsoft BASIC derivations) will search through each line in the program until it finds the right line number of the "calculate new location" step. The further away this step is from the beginning of the program, the longer the search will be; if it is very close to the beginning of the program, then the search will be shorter. The major factor in ball speed is the execution time of the update loop. Thus to obtain maximum playing speed, put the update loop as close as possible to the beginning of the program.

Now using these ideas from the last three sections, here is a sample "update loop" ball moving program.

```
10 HGR: HCOLOR=3: XOLD=140: YOLD=70
12 SCALE=10: ROT=0: SHAPE=1: S=1
14 XVEL=15: YVEL=10
20 XNOW=XOLD+XVEL: YNOW=YOLD+YVEL:
   XDRAW SHAPE AT XOLD,YOLD:
   DRAW SHAPE AT XNOW,YNOW:
   XOLD=XNOW: YOLD=YNOW: GOTO 20
```

This program will start a white ball shape (SHAPE=1 gives shape number 1) at coordinates (140,70) and move it to the right at velocity 15 and downwards at velocity 10. Note the statements in line 20 that move XNOW and YNOW into XOLD and YOLD. These statements make the new ball the old ball, and enable the loop to cycle the ball to another position.

Bouncing

The only problem with our update loop is that as soon as the ball reaches the edge of the screen it will cause a syntax error. This is because the X and Y values will go beyond the allowed values of 279 or 159. The solution is to bounce the ball when it reaches the playfield edge.

Bouncing basically consists of complementing the sign of one or the other of the pair of velocities. Which velocity to complement is dependent upon which wall the ball is bouncing off. Also, the X and Y values must be readjusted after a bounce to be back in bounds. The key to bouncing is the IF...THEN statement, which is used to check if the ball is outside of the legal boundaries and to correct the ball if so. Fig. 3-30 is the flowchart for a four-wall bounce update loop:

Here is the listing for the new update loop with wallbounce:

```
20 XNOW=XOLD+XVEL: YNOW=YOLD+YVEL
30 IF XNOW<10 OR XNOW>268 THEN
```

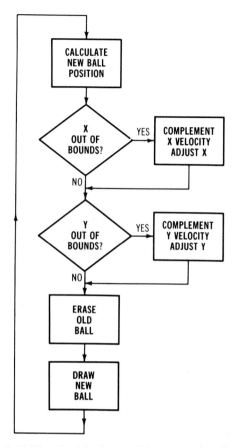

Fig. 3-30. Flowchart for four-wall bounce update loop.

```
      XVEL=-XVEL: XNOW=XOLD
40 IF YNOW<10 OR YNOW>148 THEN
      YVEL=-YVEL: YNOW=YOLD
50 XDRAW SHAPE AT XOLD,YOLD:
      DRAW SHAPE AT XNOW,YNOW:
      XOLD=XNOW: YOLD=YNOW: GOTO 20
```

We use the OR operator to check the maximum and minimum values of XNOW and YNOW. We used 10 and 268 for the X limits and 10 and 148 for the Y limits. This will keep the ball from wrapping around the screen to the opposite side. The value of XNOW and YNOW must be set to the XOLD and YOLD if either velocity complements. This is to get the ball back in the legal playfield area.

Paddles

A paddle is usually a vertical line or bar that is about one-fifth to one-eighth the vertical height of the playfield. The paddle is usually drawn at the extreme left or right border. The paddle can be another shape in the current shape table. Fig. 3-31 shows how a new paddle shape is created from 12 shape vectors and then converted to decimal values to put in the DATA statement.

On the Apple the PDL function returns a value between 0 and 255 which is proportional to the setting of a potentiometer connected to the Apple game i/o connector. Up to four pots can be attached and accessed by BASIC. The pots are numbered 0 to 3 and the function PDL(1), for example, will return a number from 0 to 255 proportional to the setting of pot No. 1.

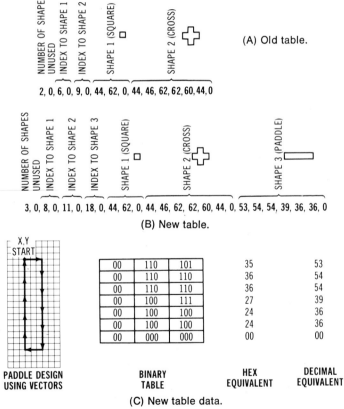

Fig. 3-31. Creating paddle shape and converting it to decimal values.

The values returned by the paddles are used for the vertical position of the paddle drawn on the screen. Since the vertical range of the outer boundary of the playfield is only 0 to 159 we must constrict the range of the paddle. This can be done by dividing the paddle value by the constant 1.6.

Also, since the SCALE for the paddle may differ from that of the ball, and since we might want to change the ROTation of the ball at some point, we should set the SCALE and ROT parameters before and after the paddle update code is executed.

Animating the paddle using PDL and the DRAW statement is basically the same as the update loop method for moving balls, and we can insert the new paddle code right inside the ball update loop. Place the new statements after the ball position is calculated, like this:

```
13 PADDLE=3: POLD=PDL(1)/1.6
20     begin ball update loop
          .
          .
          .
24 ROT=0: SCALE=5
25 PNOW=PDL(1)/1.6: XDRAW PADDLE AT 0,POLD:
   DRAW PADDLE AT 0,PNOW: POLD=PNOW
26 ROT=R: SCALE=S
          .
          .

    ball update loop continued
          .
          .
          .
```

In this program the variable R holds the rotation that was in effect before the paddles were updated, and likewise S holds the scale that was in effect before the paddles were updated. Statement 13 initializes the paddle's position POLD the first time the program is run.

We can use several methods for bouncing balls off paddles. The simple way is to simply check the ball's vertical position (YNOW) against the paddle's (PNOW) when the ball has an XNOW value of less than 10 or greater than 268. Another way is to implement a special type of bouncing where the angle of deflection is varied depending upon where the ball hits the paddle. This generates varying angles and makes the game more interesting.

Here is a listing of the game up to this point. Running it now will allow the ball to bounce endlessly inside the court. The paddle can be moved up and down to get its feel.

```
   1 HIMEM:8046
   2 GOTO 1000
  10 HGR: HCOLOR=3: XOLD=140: YOLD=70
  13 BALL=1: CROSS=2: PADDLE=3:
     SHAPE=BALL: S=10: SCALE=S:
     R=0: ROT=R: XVEL=20: YVEL=10
  14 POLD=PDL(1)/1.6: INC=2
  15 XDRAW SHAPE AT XOLD,YOLD
  20 XNOW=XOLD+XVEL: YNOW=YOLD+YVEL
  24 ROT=0: SCALE=5
  25 PNOW=PDL(1)/1.6: XDRAW PADDLE AT 0,POLD:
     DRAW PADDLE AT 0,PNOW: POLD=PNOW
  26 ROT=R: SCALE=S
  30 IF XNOW<10 OR XNOW>268 THEN
     XVEL=-XVEL: XNOW=XOLD
  40 IF YNOW<10 OR YNOW>148 THEN
     YVEL=-YVEL: YNOW=YOLD
  50 XDRAW SHAPE AT XOLD,YOLD:
     DRAW SHAPE AT XNOW,YNOW:
     GOTO 20
1000 REM LOADS THE TABLE START ADDRESS
1005 POKE 232,0: POKE 233,31: REM (8046)
1010 REM LOAD THE ACTUAL TABLE DATA
1015 FOR LOC=8046 TO 8070: READ BYTE:
     POKE LOC,BYTE: NEXT LOC: GOTO 10
1050 DATA 3,0,8,0,11,0,18,0,44,62,0,44,46,62,62,
     60,44,0,53,54,54,39,36,36,0
```

Spinning and Expanding the Ball

Since the balls for this Pong game are made of shapes we can use the SCALE and ROT statements of the Apple. ROTation can be used to make the ball seem to spin as it glides across the screen. SCALE can make the ball grow larger or shrink smaller in the middle of flight.

For demonstration purposes we will modify the program so that rotation is incremented as the ball moves. Replace statement 50 with this:

```
  50 XDRAW SHAPE AT XOLD,YOLD: R=R+INC:
     ROT=R: IF R>63 THEN R=0:
     DRAW SHAPE AT XNOW,YNOW:
     XOLD=XNOW: YOLD=YNOW
```

To make the size of the ball change on a random basis we can add a statement 60 that normally loops back to draw a new ball but 3 percent of the time allows a new scale for the ball to be generated. We will also generate new random values for the X and Y velocities, so the ball will change speed and direction when its scale is changed:

```
60 IF RND(1)<.97 THEN 20
65 XDRAW SHAPE AT XNOW,YNOW:
   S=RND(1)*20+1: SCALE=S:
   DRAW SHAPE AT XNOW,YNOW:
   XVEL=RND(1)*20+1: YVEL=RND(1)*20+1
70 GOTO 20
```

Here is a listing of the entire program as it now stands:

```
   1 HIMEM:8046
   2 GOTO 1000
  10 HGR: HCOLOR=3: XOLD=140: YOLD=70
  13 BALL=1: CROSS=2: PADDLE=3:
     SHAPE=BALL: S=10: SCALE=S:
     R=0: ROT=R: XVEL=20: YVEL=10
  14 POLD=PDL(1)/1.6: INC=2
  15 XDRAW SHAPE AT XOLD,YOLD
  20 XNOW=XOLD+XVEL: YNOW=YOLD+YVEL
  24 ROT=0: SCALE=5
  25 PNOW=PDL(1)/1.6: XDRAW PADDLE AT
     0,POLD: DRAW PADDLE AT 0,PNOW:
     POLD=PNOW
  26 ROT=R: SCALE=S
  30 IF XNOW<10 OR XNOW>268 THEN
     XVEL=-XVEL: XNOW=XOLD
  40 IF YNOW<10 OR YNOW>148 THEN
     YVEL=-YVEL: YNOW=YOLD
  50 XDRAW SHAPE AT XOLD,YOLD: R=R+INC:
     ROT=R: IF R>63 THEN R=0:
     DRAW SHAPE AT XNOW,YNOW
  60 IF RND(1)<.97 THEN 20
  65 XDRAW SHAPE AT XNOW,YNOW:
     S=RND(1)*20+1: SCALE=S:
     DRAW SHAPE AT XNOW,YNOW:
     XVEL=RND(1)*20+1: YVEL=RND(1)*20+1
  70 GOTO 20
1000 REM LOADS THE TABLE START ADDRESS
1005 POKE 232,0: POKE 233,31: REM (8046)
1010 REM LOAD THE ACTUAL TABLE DATA
1015 FOR LOC=8046 TO 8070: READ BYTE:
     POKE LOC,BYTE: NEXT LOC: GOTO 10
```

```
1050  DATA  3,0,8,0,11,0,18,0,44,62,0,44,46,62,62,
      60,44,0,53,54,54,39,36,36,0
```

Noises (Audio Output)

Most tv games that offer Pong-like play have sound effects, like the clicking sound of the ball hitting the wall, or a buzz or beep sound indicating a paddle miss. In the Apple noises can be generated from BASIC using a built-in speaker. Here is how.

Referencing location C030 hex (−16336 decimal) with a PEEK or POKE statement from BASIC will cause one-half cycle of a square wave to be sent to the speaker. Repeated references with PEEK or POKE will generate a tone with a frequency and duration determined by the frequency and number of references to the speaker. To produce a long, low buzz use this:

```
10  FOR I=1 TO 100:
    SOUND=PEEK(−16336):
    NEXT I
```

To generate a short, high-pitched click from the speaker use this:

```
20  CLICK=PEEK(−16336)+PEEK(−16336)
    +PEEK(−16336)+PEEK(−16336)+PEEK(−16336)
    +PEEK(−16336)+PEEK(−16336)+PEEK(−16336)
    +PEEK(−16336)+PEEK(−16336)+PEEK(−16336)
    +PEEK(−16336)
```

Keep in mind that the ball and paddle movement are halted during any kind of audio output (the Apple does not use built-in timer chips as the PET does), so the noises should be made as short as possible to avoid jerky movement of the ball or paddle.

Another way to generate a beep is to print a control-G (bell) using a PRINT statement. This, however, takes a lot of time and is only recommended for beeps when all the action has stopped.

Scorekeeping

A player's score can be increased each time the ball hits a brick, or when the opponent misses the ball, or any other desired condition. The score can be displayed while the game is being played. PRINT statements can be used to display the score in the lower four lines of text below the playfield. HTAB and VTAB functions can be used to automatically position the player's score in the text area, like this:

```
90 VTAB 22: HTAB 10: PRINT ASCORE;:
   HTAB 30: PRINT BSCORE;
```

Of course this assumes the text window area has been cleared first with a HOME statement.

Theory of Play

The first thing when compiling all the techniques covered in this section into a working Pong-like game is to describe in considerable detail what the game is to do, step by step. Then a flowchart must be written that includes all necessary steps (update loop, bounce effect, sound, paddles, initialize, etc.). Then the program can be written, following the flowchart, to do all the things described.

The general flow of a typical Pong game goes like this:
1. Draw playfield, initialize variables.
2. Delay in a paddle update loop to allow players to get used to the feel of the paddles.
3. Pick a random position for the ball in the center of the screen and a pair of velocities.
4. Start the update loop. Update the paddles, update the ball. Determine if the ball is going to (a) bounce, (b) miss a paddle, or (c) hit an object. If it does none of these, then return to the update loop.
5. If it hits an object or brick, then add points to the appropriate player's score, and erase the object.
6. If it misses a player's paddle, then add a point to the other player's score and erase the ball. If the other player has not won, then go back to the paddle update delay (Step 2).
7. If a player has won (has more than a fixed number of points) then acknowledge the win and end the game.

Noises and other special effects can be added at the proper places in the program.

DETAILED DRAWING AND DIGITIZING TABLES

Although high screen density means increased realism, stop for a moment and ask yourself how would you get a highly detailed drawing onto the screen of a high-resolution graphics computer? The answer is not as simple as it would seem.

Graphics Input Devices

Today there are about three different approaches to entering graphics information in a computer:

1. Keyboard Entry—The simplest method for entering graphics data is by using the keyboard and a program that lets you turn individual dots on and off or draw lines by typing in their coordinates. Obviously this approach is very time consuming, but it has the redeeming advantage of needing no extra hardware. If the computer offers shape tables like the Apple, the keyboard can be used to build shapes by specifying vectors instead of coordinates. Again this is time consuming but in some cases it may be adequate.

2. Light Pens—A light pen is a small pen-sized device that contains a light-sensitive photocell in its tip and connects to the computer via a cable. With sufficient circuitry and software the position of the pen on the screen of the computer can be determined. The limits of resolution of the light pen are set by the resolution of the screen itself. This means we can't expect much more than to be able to draw on the screen. Further, if you wish to trace a drawing with the light pen from, say, paper to the screen of the computer you must get the drawing onto clear Mylar, tape it over the screen, and then trace it out on the screen with the pen.

3. Digitizing Tables—A digitizing table consists of a flat table surface about 15 inches by 15 inches (38 cm by 38 cm) square, with a penlike device connected to it via a cable. The table contains circuits that allow it to measure the position of the pen to an accuracy of 0.005 inch (127 μm)! A typical digitizing table has an active area of 11 by 11 inches (28 by 28 cm). The digitizing table sends the computer over 100 coordinates per second and each coordinate can be a number from 0 to 2048. This not only allows extremely accurate data to be entered but means that pen motion will be fluid and smooth. With a digitizing table you can trace highly detailed drawings and have them scaled to any proportions and then echoed on the screen. You can trace the path of a trip on a map and get precise distance. You can trace out a polygon and have the area measure out super-accurately. You can even create schematics on the screen and use the pen to move logic gates, draw wires between the gates, etc. This last application is called *computer aided design*. Later a

demonstration program will be presented that will illustrate this most incredible application.

The Talos Digitizing Table

The digitizing table used in this book is made by Talos Systems and represents a good example of the state of the art for low-cost home computers. The table works with the PET 2001, the Radio Shack TRS-80, and the Apple II and costs under $450. Remember that although these devices have been used for some time in the industry, they have only recently become available for the low-cost home computers.

The Talos digitizing table consists of a flat table approximately 15 inches square and a small "pen" that is attached to the table through a cable. The "pen" isn't really a pen, but instead contains a tiny transmitting device in its tip. The tip also contains a tiny switch so the computer can tell when the pen is being pressed down on the table.

The basic job of the table is to send very accurate data to the computer that represent the position of the pen in the X,Y plane of the table. It is the job of the computer software to decide what to do with this data. This position data is usually sent to the computer many times per second.

There are several ways a digitizing table can work, but in general the pen acts like a transmitter to the table, and the table like a receiver. The table contains circuits that use the transmitted signal to accurately determine the location of the pen in the X-Y plane.

There are basically three methods for detecting pen position: sonic, magnetostrictive, and pure electronic. The Talos table used in this book uses a patented differential current measurement technique (see Fig. 3-32). The pen sends a 100-kHz signal to the table via a tiny coil in the pen tip. Under the table is a double-sided pc board with parallel lines (0.2 inch or 0.5 centimeter apart) running horizontally on one side and vertically on the other. IC amplifiers are connected to one end of each wire. The wire forms a one-turn coil to the amplifier input. Analog circuits scan the wires 100 times per second, first all the X-side wires, then all the Y-side wires. The circuits then use a special differential current subtracting technique that accurately determines the position of the pen between two wires to 0.005 inch (127 μm).

The table then sends the Apple interface (or any interface that is connected to the table) 16 bits of data: 14 bits of X or Y, a pen up or down bit, and a bit indicating if the data is X or Y.

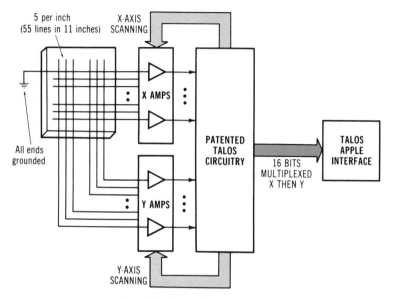

Fig. 3-32. Talos digitizing table.

The Apple interface uses 12 bits of this data, giving an overall range of 2048 points in either axis. Dividing this by 200 points per inch (about 78 per centimeter) gives a maximum range for the Talos unit of about 10.24 inches (26 cm).

Using a Digitizing Table with BASIC

In order to use the digitizing table with BASIC programs on the Apple a special assembly driver routine must first be loaded into memory. The purpose of the routine is to put the incoming data from the table into five locations in memory. The routine is called from BASIC with a CALL instruction. When the routine is called it returns two bytes of X data, two bytes of Y data, and a pen up/down byte. Our BASIC program then uses the PEEK function to convert these values to variables. First, on p. 159 is the 53-byte assembly driver routine for the Talos table.

The listing was produced using the Apple disassembler and was printed on an Axiom printer.

There are several ways to get the driver routine into memory. Considering that the routine is short (53 bytes) the best way is to convert the hex bytes to decimal equivalents in a DATA statement and then POKE them into memory with a FOR..NEXT loop.

```
0306-    AD 00 C4    LDA    $C400
0309-    AC C0 C0    LDY    $C0C0
030C-    2C 00 03    BIT    $0300
030F-    F0 F5       BEQ    $0306
0311-    29 0F       AND    #$0F
0313-    8D 01 03    STA    $0301
0316-    8C 02 03    STY    $0302
0319-    AD 00 C4    LDA    $C400
031C-    AC C0 C0    LDY    $C0C0
031F-    2C 00 03    BIT    $0300
0322-    D0 F5       BNE    $0319
0324-    AA          TAX
0325-    29 10       AND    #$10
0327-    8D 05 03    STA    $0305
032A-    8A          TXA
032B-    29 0F       AND    #$0F
032D-    8D 03 03    STA    $0303
0330-    8C 04 03    STY    $0304
0333-    60          RTS
0334-    E6 41       INC    $41
```

Courtesy Talos Systems, Inc.

The Talos digitizing table returns five bytes of data when the driver subroutine is called—two bytes of X, two bytes of Y, and a pen up/down byte. Since X and Y are each larger than 255 (the largest number possible in one byte), it is necessary to split X and Y into two bytes called XLSB (least significant bits), XMSB (most significant bits), YLSB, and YMSB. The fifth byte is called PEN, and if PEN=0, the digitizer pen is being pressed down, and if PEN=16, the pen is not pressed down, or up.

The LSB of X and Y is a full 8 bits while the MSB of X and Y is 4 bits. This is a total of 12 bits for each axis, or 2048 decimal points. The results in memory look like this after doing a CALL DIG (assuming DIG=774 and this is beginning of driver routine):

Memory Location (Base 10)	Stored There
769	XMSB
770	XLSB
771	YMSB
772	YLSB

To convert these bytes in memory to decimal coordinates for our BASIC program we use the PEEK function and a simple formula (shown here for X):

X = (PEEK(XMSB) * 256) + PEEK(XLSB)

where XMSB=769 and XLSB=770 have previously been given. The formula for the Y bytes is similar except we use YMSB and YLSB.

In order to use these values say for drawing in high resolution on the Apple we need the BASIC program to check for when the pen is pressed, read the new coordinates, and draw a line from the old coordinates to the new. We can perform a simple loop like this:

```
 50 CALL DIG IF NOT PEEK(YMSB) THEN 27000
 60 XNOW=.....formula for X
 65 YNOW=.....formula for Y
 70 RETURN
100 GOSUB 50: IF PEEK(PEN) THEN 100
                  .
          program to do something
          with new coordinates
                  .
```

Here the statement in line 100 is a GOSUB 50 that causes the driver to execute and the new X, Y, and PEN values to be placed in to memory. Next the PEEK(PEN) statement inside the IF...THEN statement checks if the PEN is up (greater than 1) or down (0). If the pen is up, the statement loops back to call the driver again. If the pen is down, then the code following the IF...THEN statement is executed, which could be HPLOT TO statements which draw a line or plot a point.

Since the returned values are as large as 2048, we must scale them by dividing each coordinate by a constant.

Using the Digitizing Table: Talos Demonstration

Using the digitizing table can best be illustrated with a demonstration program available from Talos Systems. The program is designed to run on any 16K Apple with Applesoft on ROM and a Talos DIG-I-KIT-IZER or SIMPLE-ONE.

The demonstration program for the digitizing table was written by Talos Systems and comes free with the Talos table. The program consists of six demonstrations described below. The entire demonstration program is loaded and then the bottom area of the table becomes a main menu area used to select the desired demo with the pen. Fig. 3-33 shows the table with the menu taped on.

Digitize Raw Coordinates

This program simply outputs the X and the Y coordinate values when the pen is pressed down on the table. As the pen

Fig. 3-33. Digitizing table with menu.

Courtesy John Werner

is moved about the table the numbers displayed on the screen are updated to represent the new pen position. The demonstration is useful for showing the dynamic range of the digitizing table.

Distance

This program is used to accurately measure distance, such as for trips, perimeters of property, etc. For example, a map can be placed on the table and the pen touched along the path you might travel. Each time the pen is touched on the path, the new distance accumulates at the bottom of the screen. When done you can use the map's scale factor as a multiplier to get exact miles. Keep in mind that the software has 9 digits, so you can be sure it is accurate. However, the table is only accurate to one part in 2048 or about $3\frac{1}{2}$ digits of accuracy. To check the accuracy of the table a ruler was placed on the table. A point right above the 1-inch mark was touched and then a point above the 10-inch mark was touched with the pen. The table read out the distance 8.9933125 inches!

Area

The area program is extremely useful. You can trace out any polygon or irregular closed figure and the computer will print out the exact area. See Fig. 3-34.

The program relies on a simple algorithm for calculating area of a polygon given the coordinate points for the vertices as follows:

$$\text{Area} = 1/2 \; (X1*Yn + X2*Y3 \ldots.+ Xn{-}1*Yn + Xn*Y1$$
$$- \; Y1*X2 - Y2*X3 \ldots.- Yn{-}1*Xn - YnX1)$$

161

Fig. 3-34. Use of area program.

This program can be used to calculate the cost of materials from a drawing, the area of a strange shape including curves, the area of a floor plan, and so on.

Music

This program shows how you can use the digitizing table as a music machine. The Y axis controls the pitch of the tone and the X axis controls the duration of the tone (the tone is pulsed on and then off). This rather unique application might be used in a game to teach manual dexterity. Since the pen position can be measured we have an objective measure of the user's movements. The game could be to chase the sound with the pen.

Color Painting

This is the original low-resolution graphics drawing program for the Apple that allows you to paint in low-resolution color from seven drawing colors and three screen colors. The pen is used to "dip" into the colors to select a color for painting.

Drawing

The drawing program allows you to create pictures on the screen in the high-resolution mode. Fig. 3-35 shows a map of the world in the drawing area of the hires drawing program.

A small crosshair moves about on the screen following the pen's movements on the table. When the crosshair is moved into a box in the menu area and then pushed down, the function described by that box is enabled and a duplicate image of the

Fig. 3-35. Plot of world map.

crosshair is latched in that box to indicate the function chosen. The broken line in either of the two left boxes of the menu puts the pen in the point mode, which means that when the pen is pressed points are output to the screen. The first box is for white lines and the second box for black. This is the mode for freehand drawing. The solid line in either of the next two boxes puts the pen in the line mode, which automatically draws lines between digitized points. These can be used for erasing black or white lines, or for drawing white or black lines. The last two boxes on the right select black or white backgrounds.

Once a drawing has been created in the drawing area it can be saved permanently on magnetic tape or diskette by storing the memory image from 2000 to 4000 hex (8192 bytes of screen memory in the Apple). Later you can recall the image from disk or tape for modification.

Computer Aided Design (CAD)

This is perhaps the most incredible application of the graphic computer and the digitizing table. The name of the demonstration is slightly misleading because you might think the computer does the designing. Sorry, it is not so. What the program does do is still incredible. It allows you to draw schematics on the screen of Apple in high resolution and is similar to systems sold by Calma and Calcomp.

The program is similar to the drawing program, but in addition it has a menu of electronic logic symbols including an AND gate, inverter, and OR gate. As shown in Fig. 3-36 these symbols can be used to create a detailed schematic of a logic

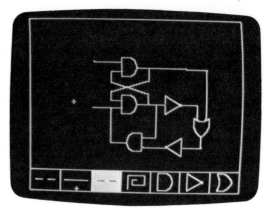

Fig. 3-36. CAD of logic circuits.

circuit. The gates can be "captured" with the pen, and moved to any place on the screen and then locked there when the pen is removed. The spiral figure in the menu area is for rotating the gates to one of four directions.

The point and line drawing functions can be chosen to connect outputs to inputs, to make connection dots, to draw resistors, and so on.

The schematic can be printed out on the Axiom EX-820 printer (a low-cost printer for the Apple) by doing a complete screen dump to the printer. Note that this is not an ordinary printer but instead contains special firmware for copying the high-resolution page.

With a little more work to the program you could have additional menus that contain analog components, resistors, capacitors, and a menu that contains labels such as Rs and Cs that can be placed on the schematic for identification.

One could create a generalized CAD program that allowed making custom shapes for the menu, such as pipe sections, engine parts, pumps and gears, and so on. The pen could be used to move the parts and stick them together as you wished— much easier than drawing by hand and erasing.

The final word would be to have the circuit we created actually start up and run! Imagine the effect this would have on technicians today.

MOVING FIGURE ANIMATION

In this section we will explore the basic concepts of animation on the computer. We shall see how to make things walk, run, and fly from BASIC. You should understand that animation on the computer is so new and so revolutionary that very few of the new home computers are capable of it. And to be sure even the Apple is not totally set up for animation from BASIC, but it's darn close. The main requirements of a computer for animation are dense display format and a high-speed BASIC. If BASIC is slow then there will be objectionable flicker, and if the screen display is not dense enough the movement will not be fluid.

First, What Is an Animation?

An animation is a series of pictures, each slightly different than the one before it, presented to the viewer at a rate fast enough to give the impression of smooth real movement. We have seen how to make a simple object move across the screen, such as the bird, by constant plotting and replotting of the object. This is very trivial animation. True animation can be illustrated by simulating a moving figure such as a running bird, walking man, and so on. With moving figure animation we must be able to present a series of pictures of the object with the elements of the object (like the limbs) slightly displaced from their previous positions. If we want total realism we should show all bends, tilts, and other subtle changes that occur as the figure moves.

There are several ways to approach this problem from the viewpoint of programming. The best approach would be to use assembly language because it is so fast, but this would be beyond the scope of this book, and only a small number of professional programmers would understand it. The next best approach, and the one used here, is to do the animation from BASIC.

Walking Animation

Consider for a moment how we walk. Our upper legs (thighs) are hinged to our hips so they swing freely. Our lower legs (calves) are hinged to our thighs at the knee, and they too swing in an arc. Finally our feet are attached to our calves so that they too swing in a small arc. In general, all legs and arms have this feature of rotation. Does this suggest a technique that might be used on the Apple to create an animation of walking?

Example 26:

Write a program that animates a walking bird (knees bend backward compared to people's) on the Apple. Use a shape table with a single vector in it to represent one of the sections a leg. Have rotation values stored in DATA statements that set the position of the legs for each frame of the animation. Have the legs divided into an upper leg hinged at the hip, a lower leg hinged at the knee, and a foot hinged at the bottom of the lower leg. Since a bird has two legs, there will be six parts, with six rotations per frame or per DATA statement.

Solution:

Obtain an Animation Source

Begin by obtaining a source of animation frames for use in the program such as the one shown in Fig. 3-37 of the bird.* If you can't find such a source, you can make cardboard figures with hinged limbs to imitate the movements.

Fig. 3-37. This was used to obtain leg positions for the bird animation program.

Convert the Source to Animation Schematic

Fig. 3-38 is a way to represent the several steps of the animation in two diagrams, each showing all the positions of a leg for the entire animation. As you can see the *A* leg follows a simple shifting motion while the *B* leg has much more extended movements.

Convert the Schematic to Rotations

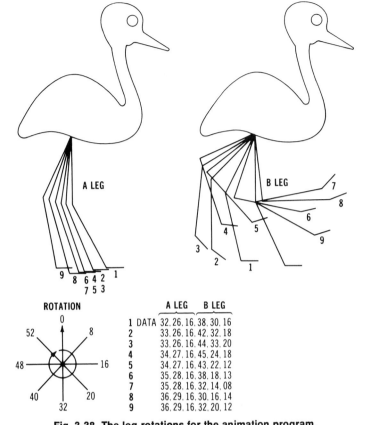

	A LEG	B LEG
1 DATA	32, 26, 16,	38, 30, 16
2	33, 26, 16,	42, 32, 18
3	33, 26, 16,	44, 33, 20
4	34, 27, 16,	45, 24, 18
5	34, 27, 16,	43, 22, 12
6	35, 28, 16,	38, 18, 13
7	35, 28, 16,	32, 14, 08
8	36, 29, 16,	30, 16, 14
9	36, 29, 16,	32, 20, 12

Fig. 3-38. The leg rotations for the animation program.

Next we convert the angled positions of the legs to numbers inside of DATA statements. The first three numbers are the A leg rotations, the next three the B leg.

Write a Program to Use This Data (see p. 168)

---

*You can find other such drawings for making animation programs in Budd Wentz' *Paper Movie Machines,* Troubador Press, San Francisco, 1975.

As you can see the program is very simple, considering what it accomplishes. It begins by setting HIMEM: to 8046. Next variables INC and MAX are initialized. INC is the number added to the bird's X position each time it moves a leg. The larger INC the faster the bird moves. MAX is the number of DATA statements in the program. S1 is set to 20 and repre-

```
0    HIMEM: 8046
1    INC = 2
2    MAX = 9
10   HGR : HCOLOR= 3:X = 140:Y = 7
     0
11 S1 = 20:S2 = 5
12   GOTO 1000
50   HPLOT X,Y: SCALE= S1: ROT= R1
     : DRAW 1: ROT= R2: DRAW 1: ROT=
     R3: SCALE= S2: DRAW 1
55   HPLOT X,Y: SCALE= S1: ROT= R4
     : DRAW 1: ROT= R5: DRAW 1: ROT=
     R6: SCALE= S2: DRAW 1: RETURN

100  FOR I = 1 TO MAX
120  READ R1,R2,R3,R4,R5,R6
130  HCOLOR= 3: GOSUB 50
135  FOR D = 1 TO  PDL (0): NEXT
     D
145  HCOLOR= 0: GOSUB 50
146 X = X + INC
150  NEXT I
155  RESTORE
160  IF X > 220 THEN X = 20:S1 =
     RND (1) * 50 + 10:S2 = S1 /
     4:INC = S1 / 8
165  GOTO 100
200  REM
201  REM
300  REM   START OF LEG MOVEMENTS
311  DATA  32,26,16,38,30,16
312  DATA  33,26,16,42,32,18
313  DATA  33,26,16,44,33,20
314  DATA  34,27,16,45,24,18
315  DATA  34,27,16,43,22,12
316  DATA  35,28,16,38,18,13
317  DATA  35,28,16,32,15,8
318  DATA  36,29,16,30,16,12
319  DATA  36,29,16,32,20,12
998  REM
999  REM   A ONE VECTOR SHAPE
1000  POKE 232,110: POKE 233,31
1010  POKE 8046,1: POKE 8047,0: POKE
     8048,4: POKE 8049,0: POKE 80
     50,4: POKE 8051,0
1030  GOTO 100
```

sents the initial scale for the upper and lower legs, while S2
is set to 5 to represent the smaller scale of the foot (remember,
we are using the same vector for the legs and feet).

The program jumps to line 1000, where the vector shape table is POKED into memory along with the starting address of the shape since we are not using SHLOAD.

Next we are sent to line 100, where the main work of the program begins with a FOR..NEXT loop. The loop causes six variables to be READ from the first DATA statement. Then the HCOLOR is made white and the GOSUB 50 is executed. This subroutine takes the six variables and uses each one as a rotation before drawing one of the legs. The subroutine starts with an HPLOT statement which determines where the upper leg will be drawn from (and hence the hips of the bird). Each part of the leg is drawn immediately after the one before it. Only scale and rotation are changed. The DRAW statement without an AT X,Y accomplishes this.

After leg *A* is drawn we draw leg *B* and leave the subroutine. The color is changed to black and the GOSUB 50 is used again, but this time to erase the legs. Then X is incremented and the loop repeats for the next DATA statement.

When all DATA statements have been executed and the loop is over, statement 160 checks the X position and if it is greater than 220 the bird is far enough right to overflow the HPLOT statement when a DRAW is executed. So we reset X to zero. To make the demonstration interesting we also use the RND statement to generate a random scale S1 so the legs will change size. S2 is made one quarter of S1 for the foot. INC, which controls speed, is made one-eighth the size of S1 so larger shapes move faster. Finally, the program jumps back to line 100 to repeat the drawing part with a new scale. Line 135 is used to put a delay in the redrawing proportional to the paddle setting so that we can manually slow down and speed up the animation.

Adding a Body Shape

At this point the animation will be a bodyless set of legs. To add a body we can define another shape in the shape table and do a DRAW 3 before drawing the legs. See Example 27.

Example 27:

Add a simple body to the bird legs using a third shape in the shape table. Store the shape vectors in DATA statements. Keep the number of vectors for the body under 50 to reduce the flicker effect.

Solution:

Draw the Body on 0.1-inch (0.25-cm) Grid Paper

As shown in Fig. 3-39 draw the bird's body as a series of up, down, right, or left vectors. Divide the vectors into logical subsections.

Convert the Body to Data Statements

Use the key for shapes (shown in Fig. 3-39) to convert the vectors to a series of numbers 0, 1, 2, or 3. These represent the vector's directions.

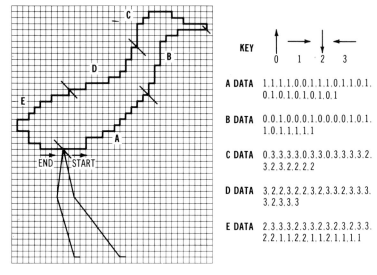

A DATA 1,1,1,1,0,0,1,1,1,0,1,1,0,1,
0,1,0,1,0,1,0,1,0,1

B DATA 0,0,1,0,0,0,1,0,0,0,0,1,0,1,
1,0,1,1,1,1,1

C DATA 0,3,3,3,3,0,3,3,0,3,3,3,3,2,
3,2,3,2,2,2,2

D DATA 3,2,2,3,2,2,3,2,3,3,2,3,3,3,
3,2,3,3,3

E DATA 2,3,3,3,2,3,3,2,3,2,3,2,3,3,
2,2,1,1,2,2,1,1,2,1,1,1,1

Fig. 3-39. The body for the bird animation program is sourced in DATA statements.

Modify the Program to Draw a Body

```
0    HIMEM: 8046
1    INC = 2
2  MAX = 9
10   HGR :X = 140:Y = 85
11   S0 = 1:S1 = 20:S2 = 5:R0 = 0
12   HCOLOR= 3
13   POKE  - 16302,0
14   GOTO 2000
50   SCALE= S1: ROT= R1: DRAW 1 AT
        X,Y: ROT= R2: DRAW 1: ROT= R
        3: SCALE= S2: DRAW 1: SCALE=
        S1: ROT= R4: DRAW 1 AT X,Y: ROT=
        R5: DRAW 1: ROT= R6: SCALE=
        S2: DRAW 1
60   SCALE= S0: ROT= R0: DRAW 2 AT
        X,Y: RETURN
100   RESTORE
105   FOR I = 1 TO MAX
120   READ R1,R2,R3,R4,R5,R6
```

```
130    HCOLOR= 3: GOSUB 50
135    FOR D = 1 TO  PDL (0): NEXT
       D
146 X = X + INC
150    NEXT I
155    RESTORE
160    IF X < 220 THEN 100
165 S1 =  RND (1) * 40 + 10:S2 =
       S1 / 4:INC = S1 / 8
166 INC = 30
170 S0 = S1 / 12: IF S0 < 1 THEN
       S0 = 1
175 X = 20
176    HCOLOR= 0: HPLOT 0,0: CALL 6
       2454
180    GOTO 100
200    REM
201    REM
300    REM   START OF LEG MOVEMENTS
311    DATA   32,26,16,38,30,16
312    DATA   33,26,16,42,32,18
313    DATA   33,26,16,44,33,20
314    DATA   34,27,16,45,24,18
315    DATA   34,27,16,43,22,12
316    DATA   35,28,16,38,18,13
317    DATA   35,28,16,32,15,8
318    DATA   36,29,16,30,16,12
319    DATA   36,29,16,32,20,12
998    REM
999    REM   A ONE VECTOR SHAPE
1000   POKE 232,110: POKE 233,31
1010   POKE 8046,1: POKE 8047,0: POKE
       8048,4: POKE 8049,0: POKE 80
       50,4: POKE 8051,0
1030   GOTO 100
2000   REM   LEG VECTOR AND BODY
2001   REM   VECTOR STORED HERE
2005   POKE 232,110: POKE 233,31
2010   POKE 8046,2: POKE 8047,0: POKE
       8048,6: POKE 8049,0: POKE 80
       50,8: POKE 8051,0: POKE 8052
       ,4: POKE 8053,0
2015   FOR DUM = 1 TO 54: READ I: NEXT
       DUM
2020   FOR LOC = 8054 TO 8191
2025   READ ASEC,BSEC
2026   IF ASEC = 9 OR BSEC = 9 THEN
       2060
2030 BYTE = (BSEC * 8) + ASEC + 3
     6
2035   POKE LOC,BYTE
2045   NEXT LOC
2060   POKE LOC,0: POKE LOC + 1,0:
       GOTO 100
```

```
2100  REM
2101  DATA   1,1,1,1,0,0,1,1,1,0,
      1,1,0,1,0,1,0,1,0,1,0,1,0,1
2102  DATA   0,0,1,0,0,0,1,0,0,0,0
      ,1,0,1,1,0,1,1,1,1,1,1
2103  DATA   0,3,3,3,3,0,3,3,0,3,3
      ,3,3,2,3,2,3,2,2,2,2
2104  DATA   3,2,2,3,2,2,3,2,3,3,2
      ,3,3,3,3,2,3,3,3
2105  DATA   2,3,3,3,2,3,3,2,3,2,3
      ,2,3,3,2,2,1,1,2,2,1,1,2,1,1
      ,1,1
2106  DATA   9,9
```

The final program is simply an extension of the previous one. To use the full screen we do a POKE −16302,0 at line 13 and then immediately go to line 2000, where the tables of the shape are POKEd in. As before, the leg vector is stored. The table header is different now because there are two shapes instead of one. Statement 2015 is a dummy loop that causes the DATA pointer to move past the leg movement vectors so it points at the beginning of the DATA statements in line 2101–2106. In line 2020 a loop is begun which reads the body data, converts it to numbers, and stores it in the shape table. The formula in line 2030 converts the numbers in the data statements to values for the shape table. Line 2026 checks for an end of table condition. When done we poke zero at the end of the table, and jump to line 100 to enter the animation routine. This part of the program works as before except we add a new statement to the drawing subroutine at line 60 to draw the body shape.

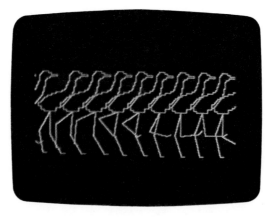

Fig. 3-40. Successive position of bird on screen.

The size of the body is S0, which is made to be one-twelfth the size of S1. Fig. 3-40 shows a typical walk of the bird across the screen.

Further Animations

We don't need to limit animation to walking or running. The same techniques used here could be used to animate a bird flying with flapping wings, a body dangling from a rope in a game of hangman, a frog jumping or catching a fly with its tongue, a tree bending in the wind, and so on, limited only by your imagination and the number of vectors in the shape.

Computer Graphics Manufacturers

American Microsystems, Inc. (AMI)
3800 Homestead Road
Santa Clara, California 95051

Apple Computer, Inc.
10260 Bandley Drive
Cupertino, California 95014

Atari, Inc.
1265 Borregas Avenue
P.O. Box 9027
Sunnyvale, California 94086

Axiom Corp.
5932 San Fernando Road
Glendale, California 91202

Bally Manufacturing Corp.
Consumer Products Div.
10750 West Grand Avenue
Franklin Park, Illinois 60131

Biotech Electronics
P.O. Box 485
Ben Lomond, California 95005

Chromatics, Inc.
3923 Oakcliff Industrial Court
Atlanta, Georgia 30340

Commodore Business Machines Ltd.
901 California Avenue
Palto Alto, California 94304

Compucolor Corp.
P.O. Box 569
Norcross, Georgia 30091

Digital Engineering, Inc.
1787 Tribute Road
Sacramento, California 95818

Digital Graphic Systems
595 Matadero Avenue
Palto Alto, California 94306

Eclectic Corp.
2830 Walnut Hill Lane
Dallas, Texas 75229

Evans & Sutherland
580 Arapeen Drive
Salt Lake City, Utah 84108

Exidy, Inc.
Data Products Div.
969 W. Maude Avenue
Sunnyvale, California 94086

Hewlett-Packard, Inc.
Data Terminals Div.
19400 Homestead Road
Cupertino, California 95014

Houston Instrument, Inc.
Div. of Bausch & Lomb
One Houston Square
Austin, Texas 78753

Intelligent Systems Corp.
4376 Ridgegate Drive
Duluth, Georgia 30136

Matrox Electronics Systems Ltd.
2795 Bates Road
Montreal, Que. H3S 1B5 Canada

Micro Diversions
8455-D Tyco Road
Vienna, Virginia 22180

Motorola Semiconductors
3501 Ed Bluestein Blvd.
Austin, Texas 78721

Radio Shack Corp.
Division of Tandy Corp.
1400 One Tandy Center
Fort Worth, Texas 76102

Solid State Sales
P.O. Box 74
Somerville, Massachusetts 02143

Talos Systems, Inc.
7419 East Helm Drive
Scottsdale, Arizona 85260

RCA VIP Marketing
New Holland Avenue
Lancaster, Pennsylvania 17604

Tektronix, Inc.
P.O. Box 500
Beaverton, Oregon 97077

Texas Instruments, Inc.
P.O. Box 1444
Houston, Texas 77001

Screen Comparisons

This appendix is presented as an aid to revealing and comparing the actual screen densities of the most popular low-cost home computers that feature graphics. In Fig. B-1 the screen outlines are drawn and the numbers of horizontal dot columns and vertical dot rows are labeled. If the dot matrix is indirectly accessible (i.e., no software instruction exists for easily turning a dot on or off) then the indirect resolution is given in parenthesis, and the character resolution is marked on the screen. If mixed graphics is allowed (that is, mixing text or graphics characters with graphics dots) then the character matrix is indicated by heavy lines around the lighter denser matrix.

Under each screen drawing is a circled enlargement of the dot matrix of the computer. These have all been drawn to the same scale so that comparisons can easily be made between them. To create the spacing for the enlargements, it was assumed that for all computers the aspect ratio of the tube was 3:4 and the actual screen dimensions were assumed to be 32 by 24 inches (about 81 by 61 centimeters). The large size was chosen for ease of calculations and doesn't represent a true size of screen. Next the spacing for the horizontal dots was determined by dividing 32 by the number of horizontal dots advertised for the computer, and the vertical spacing by dividing 24 ($32 \times \frac{3}{4}$) by the number of vertical dots advertised. For example, the 512 horizontal dots of the Exidy Sorcerer, have a $32/512 = 1/16$ inch (0.16 cm) spacing, and the vertical spacing is $24/240 = 0.1$ inch (0.25 cm).

The screen formats are reduced in the same proportion and are presented in order of increasing screen density.

Notes about the characteristics of the graphics are given when deemed necessary under the screen. The set here is not to be considered exhaustive, but represents a fair sampling of the most popular low-cost graphics-oriented computers.

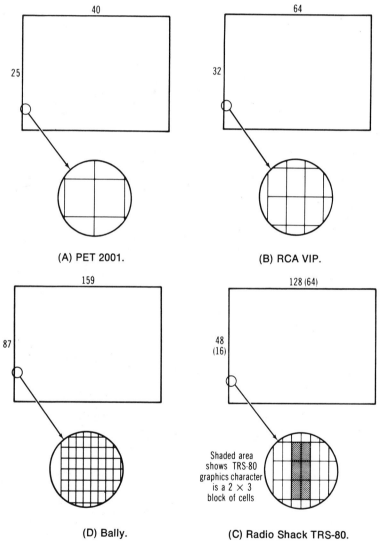

(A) PET 2001.

(B) RCA VIP.

(D) Bally.

(C) Radio Shack TRS-80.

Shaded area shows TRS-80 graphics character is a 2 × 3 block of cells

Fig. B-1. Screen

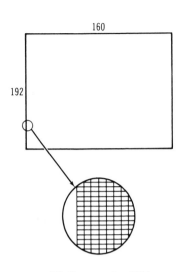

(E) Compucolor 8051.

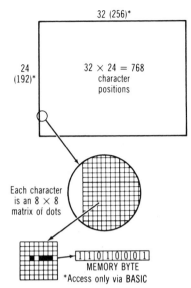

32 × 24 = 768 character positions

Each character is an 8 × 8 matrix of dots

MEMORY BYTE

*Access only via BASIC

(F) Texas Instrument TI-99/4.

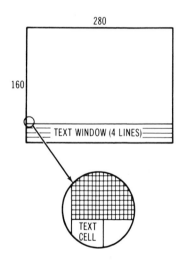

TEXT WINDOW (4 LINES)

TEXT CELL

(G) Apple II high-resolution mode.

density comparisons.

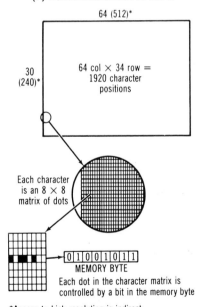

64 col × 34 row = 1920 character positions

Each character is an 8 × 8 matrix of dots

MEMORY BYTE

Each dot in the character matrix is controlled by a bit in the memory byte

*Access to high resolution is indirect through memory via BASIC pokes

(H) Exidy Sorcerer.

Index

A

Accessories, graphics, 85
Adding
  body shape, animation, 169-172
  color to the display, 39
Animation, moving figure, 164-173
  adding a body shape, 169-172
  further animation, 173
  walking animation, 165-169
  what is a, 165
Apple II
  computer profile, 55-56
  introduction to programming,
    101-103
Applesoft, 102
Architecture, 11-12
Area, programming, 161
Art, computer graphics in, 17
ASCII byte, 26
Assembly, industrial, 17
Atari
  400 computer profile, 57-58
  800 computer profile, 59-60
Automobiles, computer graphics in,
  16

B

Balls, Pong game, 146-147
Bally computer profile, 61-62
Black shapes on white backgrounds,
  135
Block graphics characters, 38
Body shape, adding a, 169-172
Borders, programming, 113
Bouncing, Pong games, 148-149
Boxes and rectangles,
          programming, 115-120

C

Calma GDS-II system, 98
Cameras, digital, 88
Cartesian equations, 103-109
Character
  generator ROM, 31-37
  graphics, expanding a ROM for,
    37-38
Chromatic CG series, 84-85
Circles, programming, 122-123
Color
  adding to the display, 39
  encoding and decoding, 39
  evaluating, 50
  graphics display, ultimate, 40-43
  painting, 162
Comparisons, screen, 177-179
Compucolor II computer profile,
  69-70

Computer
  aided design, 163-164
  graphics, 94-96
  graphics manufacturers, 174-176
COSMAC VIP computer profile,
  73-74

D

Density, screen, 50-51
Design, computer-aided, 17
Detailed drawing and digitizing
          tables, 155-164
  area, 161
  color painting, 162
  computer aided design, 163-164
  digitize raw coordinates, 160-161
  distance, 161
  drawing, 162-163
  graphics input devices, 156-157
  music, 162
  Talos digitizing table, 157-158
  using a digitizing table
    Talos demo, 160
    with BASIC, 158-160
Diagonal lines, programming, 114
Digital
  cameras, 88
  plotters, 86-87
Digitizers, image, 88-90
Digitizing table
  and detailed drawing, 155-164
  description, 85, 156
  Talos, 157-158, 160
  using with BASIC, 158-160
Display, hardware, high-density,
  45-48
Distance on digitizing table, 161
Drawing and digitizing table,
  162-163

E

Ecology, teaching, 15
Education, graphics computers in,
  14-15
Electronics, teaching, 14
Elementary gaming figures, 123-126
Equations, programming, 103-113
  Cartesian, 103-109
  polar, 109-113
Evaluating color, density, and
          screen format, 48-52
  color, 50
  density, screen, 50-51
  screen format, 51-52
Expanding a ROM for character
          graphics, 37-38
Explode program, 141

F

Falling program, 143-144
Flasher program, 144
Format, screen, 51-52
Fun and games, computer graphics
    in, 18-21

G

Games
  and fun, 18-21
  BASEBALL, 19
  LIFE EXPECTANCY, 20
  PONG, 19
  PSYCHOTHERAPY, 20-21
  Star Trek, 18-19
  TANK, 19
  US MAP, 19-20
Gaming figures, programming,
    123-135
  black shapes on white
    backgrounds, 135
  elementary, 123-126
  making a shape, 129-132
  moving the shape, 126-127
  paddle control of
    SCALE and ROTation, 134-135
    shape position, 132-134
  shape table, 127-129
Graphics
  accessories, 85
  art with shape tables, 137-145
  computer, 28-29
  hardcopy tty, 96-98
  how hard to get into, 21-24
  input devices, 156-157
  programming, 101-173
    detailed drawing and digitizing
      tables, 155-164
      area, 161
      color painting, 162
      computer aided design,
        163-164
      digitize raw coordinates,
        160-161
      distance, 161
      drawing, 162-163
      graphics input devices,
        156-157
      music, 162
      Talos digitizing table,
        157-158
      using a digitizing table:
        Talos demo, 160
      using a digitizing table with
        BASIC, 158-160
    gaming figures, 123-135
      black shapes on white
        background, 135
      elementary, 123-126
      making a shape, 129-132
      moving a shape, 126-127

Graphics—cont
  programming
    gaming figures
      paddle control of SCALE
        and ROTation, 134-135
      paddle control of shape
        position, 132-134
      shape table, 127-129
    introduction to the Apple,
      101-103
      Applesoft, 102
      graphics keywords, 102-103
    line drawing, 113-114
      borders, 113
      boxes and rectangles, 115-120
      circles, 122-123
      diagonal lines, 114
      regular polygons, 120-122
      triangles, 120
    mandalas and computer art,
      135-145
      graphics art with shape tables,
        137-145
      simple vector graphics art, 137
    moving figure animation, 164-173
      adding a body shape, 169-172
      further animations, 173
      walking animation, 165-169
      what is a, 165
    plotting, 103-113
      Cartesian equations, 103-109
      polar equations, 109-113
    writing Pong games in BASIC,
      145-155
      balls, 146-147
      bouncing, 148-149
      noises, 154
      paddles, 150-152
      playfield, 145-146
      programming the update loop,
        147-148
      scorekeeping, 154-155
      spinning and expanding the
        ball, 152-154
      theory of play, 155
      velocities and angles, 147
  non-ROM, 38-40
  screen dump printers, 94-96
  shape, 53
  software and language
    statements, 52-53
  stroke, and raster scan, 25-28

H

Hardcopy tty graphics, 96-98
Hardware, high-density display,
  45-48
Health, computer aid, 12-13
High
  -cost graphics computers, 77-85
    Chromatics CG series, 84-85
    HP 2648, 79

High—cont
Picture System II, 77-78
Tektronix 4027, 82-83
Tektronix 4051, 80-81
density display hardware, 45-48
HP 2648 computer profile, 79

I

Image digitizers, 88-90
Industry, computer graphics in, 16-17
Intercolor 8001, 67-68

K

Keyboard entry, 156
Keywords, graphics, 102-103

L

Language statements and software, graphics, 52-53
Light pen, 17, 156
Line
drawing, programming, 113-114
borders, 113
boxes and rectangles, 115-120
circles, 122-123
diagonal lines, 114
regular polygons, 120-122
triangles, 120
graphics characters, 38
Low-cost graphics computers, 54-76
Apple II, 55-56
Atari 400, 57-58
Atari 800, 59-60
Bally, 61-62
Compucolor II, 69-70
COSMAC VIP, 73-74
Intercolor 8001, 67-68
PET 2001, 63-64
Sorcerer, 65-66
TI-99/4, 75-76

M

Mandala, 50
Mandalas and computer art, 135-145
graphics art with shape tables, 137-145
simple vector graphics art, 137
Manufacturers, computer graphics, 174-176
Mathematics, teaching, 14
Matrix, character, 31-33
Memory
-mapped video, 29-31
partitioning, 43-45
Motion pictures, computers for, 13
Mouse, 17
Moving
figure animation, 164-173
Music, digitizing table and, 162

N

NASA, 11
Noises (audio output), Pong games, 154
Non-ROM graphics, 38-40

P

Paddle control, gaming figures of SCALE and ROTation, 134-135
of shape position, 132-134
Paddles, Pong games, 150-152
Partitioning, memory, 43-45
Perspectives, 9-24
how hard to get into graphics, 21-24
what is a graphics computer, 10-11
what is possible today, 14-21
art, 17
education, 14-15
fun and games, 18-21
industry, 16-17
what's been going on, 11-13
PET 2001 computer profile, 63-64
Physics, teaching, 14
Picture System II computer profile, 77-78
Playfield, Pong games, 145-155
Plotters, digital, 86-87
Plotting equations, programming, 103-113
Cartesian, 103-109
polar, 109-113
Polar equations, 109-113
Polygons, programming, 120-122
Pong games, writing in BASIC, 145-155
balls, 146-147
bouncing, 148-149
noises, 154
paddles, 150-152
playfield, 145-146
programming the update loop, 147-148
scorekeeping, 154-155
spinning and expanding the ball, 152-154
theory of play, 155
velocities and angles, 147
Printers, graphics screen dump, 94-96
Probability Machine, 51
Product profiles, 54-85
high-cost graphics computers, 77-85
Chromatics CG series, 84-85
HP 2648, 79
Picture System II, 77-78
Tektronix 4027, 82-83
Tektronix 4051, 80-81

Product profiles—cont
  low-cost graphics computers,
    54-76
    Apple II, 55-56
    Atari 400, 57-58
    Atari 800, 59-60
    Bally, 61-62
    Compucolor II, 69-70
    COSMAC VIP, 73-74
    Intercolor 8001, 67-68
    PET 2001, 63-64
    Sorcerer, 65-66
    TI-99/4, 75-76
    TRS-80, 71-72
Programming, graphics, 101-173
  detailed drawing and digitizing
    tables, 155-164
    area, 161
    color painting, 162
    computer aided design, 163-164
    digitize raw coordinates,
      160-161
    distance, 161
    drawing, 162-163
    graphics input devices, 156-157
    music, 162
    Talos digitizing table, 157-158
    using a digitizing table
      with BASIC, 158-160
    Talos demo, 160
  gaming figures, 123-135
    black shapes on white
      background, 135
    elementary, 123-126
    making a shape, 129-132
    moving a shape, 126-127
    paddle control of
      SCALE and ROTation,
      134-135
    shape position, 132-134
    shape table, 127-129
  introduction to the Apple,
    101-103
    Applesoft, 102
    graphics, keywords, 102-103
  line drawing, 113-114
    borders, 113
    boxes and rectangles, 115-120
    circles, 122-123
    diagonal lines, 114
    regular polygons, 120-122
    triangles, 120
  mandalas and computer art,
    135-145
    graphics art with shape tables,
      137-145
    simple vector graphics art, 137
  moving figure animation, 164-173
    adding a body shape, 169-172
    further animations, 173
    walking animation, 165-169
    what is a, 165

Programming, graphics—cont
  plotting, 103-113
    Cartesian equations, 103-109
    polar equations, 109-113
  writing Pong games in BASIC,
    145-155
    balls, 146-147
    bouncing, 148-149
    noises, 154
    paddles, 150-152
    playfield, 145-146
    programming the update loop,
      147-148
    scorekeeping, 154-155
    spinning and expanding the
      ball, 152-154
    theory of play, 155
    velocities and angles, 147
Pseudo-graphics, 54

R

Raster scan and stroke graphics,
  25-28
Raw coordinates, digitize, 160-161
Regular polygons, programming,
  120-122
Retro-graphics, 90-94
Right triangles, programs for, 119
ROM
  character generator, 31-37
  expanding for character
    graphics, 37-38
Rose curve, 112
Rotating fan program, 136

S

Scorekeeping, Pong games,
  154-155
Screen
  comparisons, 177-179
  density, 50-51
  dump printers, graphics, 94-96
  format, 51-52
Shape
  gaming figure
    black on white background,
      135
    making a, 129-132
    moving the, 126-127
  graphics, 53
  table, gaming figures, 127-129
Slinky program, 138
Software and language statements,
  graphics, 52-53
Sorcerer computer profile, 65-66
Snowflake program, 143
Spinning and expanding ball, Pong
  games, 152-154
Statements, vector graphics, 53
Stroke graphics and raster scan,
  25-28

T

Table, digitizing, *see* Digitizing table
Talos digitizing table, 157-158
Tektronix
  4027 computer profile, 82-83
  4051 computer profile, 80-81
TI-99/4 computer profile, 75-76
Triangles, programming, 120
TRS-80 computer profile, 71-72
Tty graphics, hardcopy, 96-98

U

Ultimate color graphics display, 40-43
Update loop, Pong games, programming, 147-148

V

Vector graphics
  art, simple, 137
  description, 26
  statements, 53
Velocities and angles, Pong games, 147
Video
  display generator (vdg), 41-43
  memory-mapped, 29-31
Vortex program, 142

W

Walking animation, 165-169
Writing Pong games in BASIC, 145-155